CONVERSATE
IS
NOT
A
WORD

CONVERSATE IS NOT A WORD

GETTING AWAY FROM GHETTO

JAM DONALDSON

Lawrence Hill Books

Library of Congress Cataloging-in-Publication Data
Donaldson, Jam.
  Conversate is not a word : getting away from ghetto / Jam Donaldson.
    p. cm.
  Includes index.
  ISBN 978-1-55652-780-7 (pbk.)
    1. African Americans—Race identity. 2. African Americans—Psychology.
3. African Americans—Social life and customs. 4. African Americans—
Social conditions. I. Title.

E185.625.D66 2010
305.896'073—dc22

2009042277

Cover design: TG Design
Cover images: iStockphoto/ProArtWork (ruby ring), iStockphoto/Neotakezo
(bracelets), iStockphoto/ProArtWork (earring), iStockphoto/Shunrei (silhouette),
Getty/Digital Vision collection/Christopher Robbins (necklaces)
Interior design: Sarah Olson

Published by Lawrence Hill Books
An imprint of Chicago Review Press, Incorporated
814 North Franklin Street
Chicago, Illinois 60610
ISBN 978-1-55652-780-7
Printed in the United States of America
5 4 3 2 1

I dedicate this book to my mom and dad. Thank you for giving me life and thank you for making it great (I stole that from the Golden Girls). My dad is dead so he probably won't read it, but my mom thinks it's quite groovy and she's so awesome.

I also want to sincerely thank Your Honor. You started the ball rolling. Thank you for noticing. I hope I never disappoint you. Secret: I actually like yoga very much.

CONTENTS

PROLOGUE

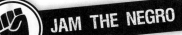

JAM THE NEGRO

"Getting away from ghetto"? I should have known this would be some patronizing manifesto on "those" black people. The "others." The people you try to forget that you are a part of. Look, SISTA, I'm not sure what you're all about, and I'll reserve my full wrath until after I read this book, BUT you clearly have issues with black people. First, you create an offensive Web site called hotghettomess.com that exploits black people and perpetuates the very stereotypes we have been trying to get away from for 400 years. Then you produce that God-awful *We Got to Do Better* show that makes us all look like buffoons. What is with you and what do you have against the ghetto? Why is *ghetto* automatically bad?

Some of our great leaders came out of the ghetto. Amazing cultural innovations and grassroots movements have come out this ghetto that you are suddenly so ashamed of. All you bourgeois black folks turn your noses up at the ghetto, at the same time blasting Biggie and Jay-Z in your Range Rovers. You heard of Michael Jackson? The Supremes? Products of the ghetto. Newsflash: Martin Luther King Jr. wasn't in Jack and Jill. Some of the greatest minds of our generation came from the ghetto. The ghetto is a place. That's it. Like any other neighborhood, you have the good, the bad, and the ugly. There is no need to paint the ghetto and everyone in it with a broad brush. Everyone doesn't have to be the Obamas in order to be good folks. So before you start talking about garbage and grammar and fried chicken and hip-hop and hardworking brothers and sisters or whatever you feel like criticizing now, I just want to go on the record saying that I'll be watching every word on every page and will call you on any bullshit you spew. You have the nerve to judge what the brothas and sistas are watching and listening to and what they're doing in their own homes? Someone is "ignorant" or "ghetto" just because they don't like what you like? Because they're not listening to NPR or watching the *Newshour*? That's outrageous, and I am so sick of your kind assuming someone is less than because they may live differently than you do. There's nothing worse than someone exploiting hard-working, God-fearing families just to make a buck. I mean, who are you to say "conversate" is not a word? There are plenty of words that people use that just take a while for mainstream society to accept. Look at "bling" or "googling." Those weren't words at first, but now they're in the dictionary. Are you suddenly the language police? As if you've never split an infinitive or misused the King's English. Sorry if the rest of us don't sound like *Masterpiece Theater*. That doesn't make someone a bad person or dumb or uncivilized. But here you are, feeling like you can get up and say whatever you want about black folks. People like you merely set the whole community up for embarrassment and ridicule. Get over yourself. But like I said, my mind is open, and I'm willing to hear you out. Please don't make me regret it.

JAM THE AMERICAN

It's about time someone had the balls to stand up and challenge some of the real, unspoken, destructive issues plaguing the African American community. No one is condemning the ghetto as a *place*; the condemnation is of ghetto as a mentality, a goal, a lifestyle glorified by mainstream media. We have stopped using excellence as a standard and started using rap videos, libidos, and daytime television as guides for how to live. Have you looked out your window lately? Have you seen how young people are representing themselves when they leave the house? And adults are just as bad. Do you see how we're living, what we're listening to, how our kids are being raised? That's what hotghettomess.com is about. It's about saying THIS SHIT IS UNACCEPTABLE. SHAME ON YOU. HGM wags a finger at all those that choose to bring the whole community down with their foolishness. Remember shame? No one seems to remember the days when you were actually ashamed to have a bunch of kids with different fathers (hell, now they'll go on TV to locate the dad). Men were ashamed when they could not provide for their families. There was a day when the only reason you dropped out of high school was to work to support your household. Education was important; family was important. Those were the two forces driving our ability to overcome the racism and discrimination we faced as a community. We had communal dreams and communal rules. But now anything goes, and shame has been all but forgotten. And this attitude is destroying so many of the gains we made in the last 100 years. Can anyone really look at the community and be satisfied with where our education, family, and community values are? Are we satisfied with how we are spending our money or using our ample resources? Are we pleased with our physical health as a community? What about our attitudes, our sense of entitlement? Or our children's attitudes and *their* sense of entitlement? I don't think any of us can look at these areas and say, "Yup, we're right on track!" So why not talk about it? Why do we have to pretend for the world that everything is OK? Why do we have to pretend that many communities are not rotting away from the inside? Why must we pretend that a get-over-gimme-I'm-entitled-to mentality has not infected many of our people? We must fix this, if only for the next generation, who won't ever know the Harlem Renaissance, the civil rights movement, or hip-hop before bitches and hos. We must get back to what made us strong, what made us survivors, what made us thrive as a community.

We are so busy trying to be ghetto fabulous, we forgot how to be great. And it's OK. We can actually have these hard, uncomfortable conversations with each other without anyone being the "bad guy." We're all adults here. How else do we solve our problems except through frank conversations with each other? Do I REALLY care about the word "conversate"? It's not about a word at all. It's about us. It's about excellence. No one is saying you must speak and act correctly at all times, but unfortunately, lots of us don't know when the hell those times are anymore or exactly what speaking and acting correctly mean. And worse, they don't care. There is a time and place for everything. And lately, many of us don't seem to know either. THAT's what this book is about. Of course, there is racism and inequality of opportunity, but how can we fight the big fights without a strong community foundation? How can we effect change in the nation when we can't even control what's going on in our own homes and neighborhoods? There are so many things that we CAN control in our lives and in our communities that it is insanity not to try to work these things out together. You can all walk around with your heads up your asses if you want to, but I'd like to see some shit get accomplished by the end of this book. Unlike you, I'm not afraid of criticism. Sometimes someone needs to shake you real good and real hard to get you out of your own self-delusions of grandeur. So just relax. Put your red-black-and-green flags down, move your *Madea* DVDs over to the side, pick out your 'fro, tell your white woman good night, close the latest Zane novel, rub on some African oils, listen up, and try to learn something for a change.

INTRODUCTION:
I'M NO REVOLUTIONARY—
HA-HA DAMN

"My hobby is stirring up Negroes." —*Malcolm X*

My father would be kicking the sides out of his coffin, if I hadn't had him cremated. His little girl, his bouncing bundle of joy for whom he set out a table of fruit at his office to celebrate her birth, is now the queen of all that is hot, ghetto, and messy. Believe me, this is just as unexpected an appointment to me as it is to anyone else. At this stage of my life, I thought I'd be married, coaching girls' soccer, and anchoring the local news. But alas, we all have our callings, and my path, although a twisted, sordid one, is my own. Telling it like I see it may be dirty work, but somebody (other than Bill Cosby) has to do it.

Let me start by straightening some things out and giving you a formal introduction. I've been called everything from a self-righteous bitch to an Uncle Tom to a money-hungry chickenhead to a revolutionary. (By the way, should "chickenhead" be hyphenated? Not sure.) And while I

1

may have a little self-righteous bitch in me, I'm certainly no revolutionary. I just say what many think and could care less what people say about me. For better or worse, the death of my dad in 2004 gave me the gift of fearlessness.

Who I am and why I do what I do has been the subject of more speculation than Beyoncé's real hair. I have been accused of being a right-wing race traitor, a misguided exploiter, child pornographer (huh?), a self-hating victim of our white supremacist society, out of touch with my roots and history, and a hot babe. Though hot babe is debatable, the rest is way off base. Is it that hard to believe that, at my core, I am an Average Joe? That I am a standard, middle-class black chick who one day stopped, looked around her, and thought, *What the hell is going on in my community*? Or is it just easier to believe that I have complex, multi-layered, nefarious motives? Why are my heartfelt concern and disgust at how my community sometimes behaves more difficult to accept than my being the tool of some right-wing conspiracy? Perhaps acknowledging that my views and concerns are sincere means you actually have to listen to what I'm saying? Is that why so many attempt to write me off as some self-hating wack job? We don't want to face what I'm saying. We don't want to think about what I'm saying. We have no answers. Well, the truth hurts. It's uncomfortable; it's embarrassing. But running away from the truth is killing us.

Contrary to popular opinion, I love my people, and because I love them, I've always been willing to dole out a big, hot, heaping spoonful of hot ghetto tough love. It just so happened, like it or not, that it became my life. So just how did I go from innocent law student, weighing the merits of corporate practice versus public interest law, putting on a Kwanzaa show for the student body, and interning as a law clerk in the U.S. Attorney's Office, to reigning queen of hot ghetto mess? Two words: not sure.

It was sort of like that moment in *Falling Down* when Michael Douglas goes berserk or that mythical time when Marvin Gaye finally hollered and threw up both his hands. Well, I had a moment like that my second year of law school at Georgetown. That moment changed my life.

Like most students, my laptop computer had become an append-age—my constant companion, my best friend. A distraction in boring law classes and a way to escape my very painful home life. My dad was dying. He had prostate cancer that had metastasized, and being his only adult child, I was his sole caregiver. I moved in with my father to take care of him. It was a very stressful time in my life, and I coped by drinking too much, experimenting with drugs, and getting lost in my computer screen.

On that screen I started to notice a disturbing trend. Well, truth be told, it wasn't disturbing at first. It was funny as hell. Many of my friends, and everyone else within six degrees of separation (except Kevin Bacon), began to send around "ghetto" pictures for fun. And like the rest of my friends, I typically would laugh my ass off. The hair weave done in the shape of a helicopter, color-coordinated pimps and hos, prom students in pasties, bedazzled pimp cups, cars with chandeliers and Burberry-pattern paint jobs. Although they are now Internet classics, back then they were novel and great material for folly. It's what we did on the Internet before YouTube. People would create elaborate Power-Point slide shows titled "Wedding in the Projects," "Fight at a Funeral," and the oft used "Look at Your Mama." Everyone would try to one-up everyone else with the funniest ghetto picture. And we just had a ball with it. A bunch of professionals and students sitting at computers all day passing these pics around like a virtual blunt and laughing just as hysterically as if the weed were real.

And one day, it just wasn't funny anymore.

I think it was somewhere between the woman in the T-shirt that proudly read "Pregnant Pussy Is the Best Pussy" and the eight-year-old boy simulating sex with a grown woman that I suddenly stopped laughing. All of a sudden, I couldn't believe that I ever thought any of this stuff was funny (even if it was just two minutes ago). I stopped everything, shut down the laptop, and asked myself, "What in the hell is going on in our communities?" And because I was in law school, I made it a two-part question: "And why are we laughing at it?" I may not have known exactly what a tort was, but I did know one thing for sure—those pictures were no longer funny.

And so began the intense renewal of my relationship with my people—with our images, our culture, our behavior, and what role we play in how the world views us and how we view one another.

I was suddenly seeing everything in a new, though admittedly dim, light. I was confused. It seemed that all my ideals and assumptions about my people and our struggles were being challenged. There was an uncomfortable paradigm shift taking place in my mind. As hard as I tried, I couldn't quite understand how what I was seeing in my community was somehow society's (read: "white people's") fault. And if it wasn't their fault, whose was it? (Cue dramatic music here.) It was ours. And only we could fix it.

Sure, the economic disparities and educational inequalities that African Americans continue to face in the United States can certainly be argued as the vestiges of Jim Crow laws and slavery, but I couldn't, no matter what intellectual gymnastics I tried, figure out why we weren't responsible for the images I was seeing every day. We're talking about basic decency and values here. I mean, did Whitey send your daughter to the prom with her tittays hanging out? No, you did. And the rest of us just stood around and laughed.

The argument that the current plight of the black community is the result of white racism and the systematic oppression of the Negro is a tricky one. If the precarious state of black America today is a direct and continuing result of a white supremacist government, then can someone please explain to me why my parents' generation was so damn classy? Why, in a generation that was closer in proximity to slavery and segregation, did the community exhibit *more* of a work ethic, more of a focus on education, more focus on family, and more pride in its image?

We have more opportunities today than that generation ever could have dreamed of, yet we are failing to uphold all these basic tenets of a strong and successful American community.

How could I argue with any integrity at all that my generation had suddenly lost its way because of slavery and the white man? Oh God! Was I becoming a conservative? Was I becoming a Republican? Was I becoming (gasp) Armstrong Williams? Were there others who thought the same way I did? I felt compelled to start the conversation. But where would I fit in?

I would listen to men like Bill Cosby, Cornel West, Roland Martin, and Michael Eric Dyson, who dominate the airwaves when it comes to issues facing the black community, and wonder, *Where are the women like me? Don't we have something to say?* I find the conspicuous absence of females in the realm of public debate on race and culture disappointing and disconcerting. Perhaps we're just too busy holding our communities together with Scotch tape to go on speaking tours. The discourse on urban issues has begun to resemble the black church: the women do all the work, but the men have all the power.

I wasn't a scholar. I wasn't a professor. I wasn't a celebrity. I wasn't on the front lines of the civil rights movement. I was just your Average Joe-Quita who happened to have an opinion and could string a couple of sentences together. And frankly, I think that's enough. In fact, too often the conversation on issues affecting the black community is dominated by professional mouthpieces, and the voices of the average man and woman get lost.

What do those who aren't professors at prominent universities think? What do people who don't have PhDs think? Yes, you can get them roused up at the State of the Black Union or some such event, but when the furor dies down and they leave those halls and go back to their living rooms and barber shops and are confronted with the reality of their daily lives, what do they *really* think? Well, I can't speak for them, but I can speak for me.

Don't get me wrong, I have great respect for our prominent academics, pundits, and activists. These people are brilliant, entertaining, compelling speakers, but we can't forget the value of common voices. I just want to make sure that as many perspectives as possible are at the table. There is an extraordinary diversity of experiences in our community. There is economic, geographic, political, religious, cultural, generational, and philosophical diversity among us, and no one should ever be left out of the conversation.

So where was I? Oh, explaining why the opinion of an average, thirtysomething, middle-class black chick with a dog named Albert and a slight case of eczema has any value at all. Moving on . . .

For me, an '80s baby, the world of the civil rights movement seemed an eternity away. That had been the Golden Age of Protest. A master class in civil disobedience. The goals were clear and common, the people generally united, and the cause noble. It was a time when there were causes greater than oneself.

So now here I am in the 21st century. Common goals have morphed into individualism. *Brown v. Board* is the distant past for most. Unlike our parents, we grew up integrated and watching *The Cosby Show*. Wanting more for us than they had, our parents regaled us with tales of opportunity. We were told we could be whoever we wanted and that there were no limits. Generations before us had sacrificed their lives so we could live the American dream. This generation doesn't know protests or sit-ins or lynchings. We know *House Party* movies and *Good Times* and hip-hop. The Rodney King beating seems like an aberration; racial profiling an inconvenience. Most of us never had to fight for anything. Generally, our lives are pretty good.

This certainly isn't to say that we aren't aware of racism, but do our protestations over cab rides denied, Mumia Abu-Jamal, and crack sentencing touch our collective black souls like integration and civil rights? Unfortunately not. Sure, we can talk until the cows come home about hip-hop and the n-word and driving while black and *Flavor of Love*, but it all seems so banal compared with the civil rights movement. And this lack of a common condition, a common enemy, a common cause, has fragmented our communities into oblivion. We were so quick to celebrate what we gained, we never stopped to think what we lost. And what we lost would become my mission. OK, my obsession. Meanwhile my dad was almost dead.

I wasn't doing this to be some kind of asshole or to be provocative for provocation's sake. I *really* thought that the solutions to some of the problems plaguing our communities might be found in the conversations we could have about our role in how the world sees us. Our role in the state of our communities. It's like the movie *Soul Food*. I just wanted the whole family to come to the table with some collards and ribs and talk honestly with one another. And I would be the Big Mama at the head of the table. Because my mission was not about trivial fashion mistakes. It wasn't about being ageist or classist. It was about recognizing what was in front of our faces: a community that has become dominated by negative influences. And the effects are devastating.

I decided to use our own images to challenge our notions of ourselves. Not Hollywood's images or the music industry's images, but images we take of one another, images we pose for and display with pride. These pictures are like a hieroglyphic tale of our downward spiral. They show the hypersexualization of our young women, our obsession with thug living and ho life. The images that came across my computer screen were walking, talking, booty-shaking examples of a generation that has lost its way. And I was determined not to let us get away with it. They show our rabid consumerism, our lack of focus on work and family, and just a general losing of the damn mind. Like the test to see if pasta is done, I was gonna throw all these images on the wall and see what stuck.

Eric Holder, the first African American Attorney General for the United States, once stated that America was a "nation of cowards" when it came to issues of race. He was right. Everyone is scared shitless to have honest discussions that involve race, and the conversations end up dominated by the loudmouths at the extremes. We tap dance around race, afraid someone will think we are racists or Uncle Toms. But too often you *will* be called a racist or an Uncle Tom if you express any opinion besides the one that happens to be politically correct at the time. Even when then-candidate Barack Obama spoke to a mostly black audience about the responsibility of fathers to play a role in their children's lives, Jesse Jackson said he wanted to cut his nuts off. I mean, is there anyone who would disagree with what Obama said? Who the hell needs Jesse cutting off nuts just for speaking the truth?

So most of us just say the hell with it and relegate our conversations to hushed tones among friends. And the conversation continues to be dominated by those on the far left or the far right, when most of us are somewhere in between. Meanwhile, the concerns, issues, conflicts, solutions, and analyses that we come up with among ourselves just continue to smolder because they are never given the oxygen of a public forum. It's a virtual race gag order. Certain things just cannot be spoken of in public (read: "in front of white people"). Life was short, my dad was dying, and all of a sudden I didn't care about the gag order anymore.

I decided the Internet, which has managed to replace money as the root of all evil, would be my conduit for a conversation I wanted desperately to have with my beloved people. I would give public voice to all those cell-phone convos and DMV-line venting sessions and IM rants. The gag was coming off. Now I needed a name.

I struggled to think of a name for my new Web site, my new mission: using images of ourselves that *we* promulgate and promote to start discussions about the state of our communities. See, these weren't images I scrounged from boxes of private photos under people's beds. These were photos that individuals had placed on the Internet with pride. Men and women posed for these pictures or took them of themselves. And the fact that people, especially young people, were proud of these images was an indication that there was definitely trouble in River City. How can we rail against negative stereotypes in the media yet at the same time choose to perpetuate these images ourselves? I wanted to talk about it.

My first choice of a name for this new site was we'redoomed.com, but I wasn't sure if Web site names could have apostrophes, which would make the were/we're thing just too confusing. The next name I decided on was real trouble: not many people know this (which is no accident), but the original title of the site was niggamess.com. For those of you unfamiliar with the term "nigga mess," I'm afraid I won't be much help. "Nigga mess" is like pornography: you can't define it, but you know it when you see it. I have often tried to think of a definition, but no words ever seem quite adequate. It's a term that my peer group and I often use to describe people, places, things, and sometimes weddings.

But I knew a site named niggamess.com would never do. People would be so up in arms about the name that its purpose and message would be absolutely lost in the mandatory n-word firestorm. Remember when the NAACP made a big show of burying the n-word? They had a whole fake burial and fake coffin and everything. All they needed were some MLK fans, "Amazing Grace," and a woman passing out down front.

So what could I call it? I needed a term that would resonate within the community. Some colloquialism that most black folks could relate to on some level. A virtual inside joke. See, the site is my communication with my community. It's a conversation about unpleasant things, topics that make us uncomfortable. It's like telling a friend that her breath is funky. It's never a pleasant conversation, but it's absolutely necessary.

So I got together with some friends and family (no doubt a dubious brain trust) and had some brainstorming sessions to come up with an appropriate title for my new crusade. We went through hotassmess .com, areufuckingkiddingme.com, and heavenhelpus.com. In the end, the winner was hotghettomess.com. Doesn't exactly roll off the tongue, but it does get the point across.

So it was time to implement a new movement. Call it Civil Rights 2.0. It was time to use high technology to inspire high-mindedness. I was going to take the Internet where it had not gone before: inside the private conversations the black community had at home, at the grocery store, in the barber shop, at church, in groups at the clubs, on the bus, and on the corners. This site would be about starting a conversation that would shock, awe, and (I hoped) inspire. I wanted to bring a movement for change working from the inside out.

I would take a generation whose primary concerns were bling, getting ahead, and getting over and force them into a conversation with a generation that worked hard, sacrificed, and died so we could have the luxury of bling, getting ahead, and getting over. We've come too far for me to sit idly by while our young women go to proms looking like hookers, applauded by their parents, who, in some cases, made the outfits.

In my own crass, unpolished way, I would promote an intracommunity civil rights movement. As in: we have the right not to act like idiots, so let's use it. Our community would feel the pangs of birth into the 21st century, prompted by the virtual Pitocin of the Internet and a smart ass.

So how would my movement-of-one fare? Maybe I was being too idealistic. Maybe I should've thought this through a bit. I looked at the backlash Cosby faced when he dared speak out against urban pathologies and a culture gone wrong. Everyone went apeshit in public while secretly agreeing in private. It wasn't that what he said wasn't true (although there were a couple of wacky generalizations and something derogatory about the name Mohammed), it was just that he said it in public.

It's still taboo to criticize the community in public. Not that I don't understand it. When a community has been beaten down like we have for the last 400 years, the last thing you want to see is some uppity Negro telling you everything you're doing wrong. But drastic times call for drastic measures.

So, would I be heard? And if I was heard, would I be taken seriously? And if I was heard and taken seriously, would anyone really care? Would everyone hate me? Would I be greeted as a liberator? And most important, didn't I have a torts exam I needed to be studying for?

In the journey to follow, my freshman-year-dorm-room-HBCU-black-power self would meet my conservative-personal-responsibility-right-leaning-get-off-your-black-ass-and-get-a-job self. There's a quote attributed to Winston Churchill: "If you're not a liberal when you're 25, you have no heart. If you're not a conservative by the time you're 35, you have no brain." Well, I was about to find out what happens when the twain doth meet. And knowing my black community, it wasn't going to be easy.

Was I wrong to do this? Was I elitist? Insensitive? Misguided? Innovative? Revolutionary? Mean? Thoughtful? A big fat idiot? At times, I wasn't sure my damn self. But I knew my motives were pure, and I cared too much not to try.

Is this the complicated duality DuBois spoke of? Shouldn't the most important thing be being a good Negro? Telling a bunch of my brothas and sistas (see, it doesn't count unless you use the "-as") that they need to get their shit together—that's not being a good Negro? But what about being a good neighbor, citizen, child, sibling, role model? Isn't that important, too? How could I be a good black person and be a good *real* person at the same time? Well, I would soon find out. Never did I expect what would actually happen when the black-power fist met a grande, skinny, double shot of the American dream.

Hotghettomess.com was born the month my dad died.

1

DUALITY:
THE WAR WITHIN

"One ever feels his twoness—an American, a Negro; two souls, two thoughts, two unreconciled strivings; two warring ideals in one dark body, whose dogged strength alone keeps it from being torn asunder."

—W. E. B. DuBois

Funny how you go from dorm-room revolutionary your freshman year, loudly singing the praises of Frances Cress Welsing and Anthony Browder until the wee hours of every morning, to "Can I just get the fuck out of here and get a job?" Black Power revisited as capitalist reality. Hear me out . . .

College is something like your mother's advice: you don't realize until you are well into adulthood that she was generally right about everything. The same with college—you don't actually realize how much you learned until well after the graduation ceremony. I never appreciated the life lessons that college taught me until much later in my adulthood.

In every African American studies class in every college in the country, you are required to read a litany of black classics. We read DuBois, Woodson, Achebe, Wright, Ellison—you know, the standard who's who of prolific black writers. So like most students in the class, I struggled to stay awake, read the CliffsNotes, cut and pasted together some paper about symbolism at the end of the semester, and prayed to pass the final. (And I had the nerve to proudly declare to anyone who would listen that I was an African American studies major.) It's actually pretty pathetic.

However, 10 years later (OK, maybe 15), as I try to navigate the complicated world of being black in the second decade of the 21st century, after being buried somewhere deep in my subconscious, the words of W. E. B. DuBois have begun to resurface. The concept of duality that he articulated, which once was only a vague, unrelatable theory, has suddenly become my reality. It's a force so strong in my life now, I cannot believe I ever ignored or dismissed it. I used to see it as a distant sentiment, irrelevant. Now, it's all I know.

I am a walking, talking, blogging personification of that duality. Everything for me is a struggle with that duality, that Negro, that American. The conflict between the two guides my life, surreptitiously informing my views and decisions and every move. Those fierce dueling beings—boy, are they a pain in the ass.

Every day I am forced to navigate the netherworld between being an American and being a Negro. And sometimes those views are at absolute odds with each other. Diametrically opposed. A philosophical stalemate. That's where I exist, and I'm not afraid to admit it. For example, this is one of my daily internal dialogues:

JAM THE NEGRO

Are you gonna try to bring the great W. E. B. DuBois into this to try to justify your self-hatred? Do you think he would approve of what you do? That's what all you confused bourgeois blacks do, try to justify your elitism by picking and choosing a few carefully selected theories so you won't feel so bad about selling your entire race down the river. Any black person that chooses to speak out against his or her community can suck it, as far as I'm concerned. This country has put us in a position of being a permanent underclass by limiting our educational and professional opportunities and manipulating our image to the world so that across the globe we are all seen as rappers and hoochies. And you want to blame us for that? We don't control the media. The media are determined to make us look like a bunch of fools and coons. You must have lost your cotton-picking mind. No pun intended.

And gurus and Web sites that pretend to be helping us, like hotghettomess.com? They are misguided tools of The Man or the products of self-deluded, self-hating fools. Chris Rock talking about the difference between black folks and niggas? He may have gotten a few laughs with that nonsense, but it was embarrassing and no doubt set black folks AND niggas back 30 years. When will we see that making fun of ourselves isn't cathartic and isn't productive—it's just plain stupid.

It's outrageous for someone to come out and embrace this "blaming the victim" mentality. Just like Bill Cosby and his wild, reckless generalizations. Him and Shelby Steele and their fancy degrees and educations and big words and

uppity attitudes. Who do they think they are? Don't they realize their successes are the exception and not the rule? How
dare they speak to lower-income communities and suggest
that they are responsible for their own conditions after years
of inequality of opportunity? There are so many forces out
there that denigrate the black image and portray the black
community in a negative light, why should our own brothers and sisters add to the oppression we already face in this
country? Why perpetuate these stereotypes? Why hold black
men and women up for ridicule and chastisement when they
are just victims of an exploitive society that holds their lives
in low regard? Shouldn't their brethren be a source of support
and encouragement? They are denied equality of opportunity
in education and health care. The community that should be
reaching back to help its brothers and sisters just looks back
and points and laughs and says, "Get off your black asses and
get a job!" It's outrageous. Institutional racism is alive and
well. I don't care if we do have a black president; there is bias
and prejudice in every aspect of our lives. To act like all of a
sudden someone waved a magic wand and "poof!" we're in a
color-blind society is ridiculous and dangerous. You and people like you are just self-righteous wannabes who clearly have
an issue with self-esteem. Perhaps your mission should be to
study your history and gain some knowledge of self instead of
telling everyone else what they should be doing.

JAM THE AMERICAN

Look, I'm as black as they come, but sometimes I'm "Power to the people, Free Mumia, Reparations now, and Love, peace, and soul," and other times I'm like, "Slavery is over, stop whining, stop begging, master capitalism, raise your kids, and keep it moving."

All I'm saying is that I want all of us to be the very best we can be, and some of that starts by taking a long look at the man in the mirror and figuring out how we can improve our lives and the lives of those around us. You can have your media and government and Illuminati conspiracy bullshit, but, if we buy into that, outside of some armed, black folk revolution, we are buying into a permanent state of victimhood. I just don't buy it. In fact, that type of thinking is so destructive. It gives everyone a reason not to even try because the deck is so stacked against them by the global anti-blackness conspiracy that any effort to improve conditions is futile. No, I just don't buy it.

Why is it so hard to believe that a person can want progress and prosperity for her community and let her people have it at the same time? We are so obsessed with this "what will white people think" mentality that we are willing to stand by silently and allow all types of destructive behavior to pervade our communities. As Dr. Phil would say, "How's that working for us?"

Unlike the generation that preceded us, this generation sits idly by and complains. We complain that we get fired because we're black, when perhaps it was that we were late every day. We complain about substandard schools yet have little involvement in our own children's education.

Meanwhile, our families are in shambles, we are vapid consumers of bullshit, our work ethic is in the toilet, and then we want to blame everyone else when our lives fall apart.

The days of the benevolent white man are over—the cavalry is not gonna rush in and save us from ourselves. The new civil rights movement will come from within the black community because all we got is us. And, after the success of Barack Obama, white people ain't gonna wanna hear shit about what we can't do and why. Newsflash: no one cares anymore. The white man didn't give you three different fathers for your children. It's the 21st century, and now's the time to take advantage of opportunities, embrace excellence, and dedicate yourself to success. So I absolutely agree with the likes of Bill Cosby and Juan Williams—it's about time someone from within has the balls to challenge the black-thought PC police and tell it like it is. Yes, the truth hurts, but the truth is exactly what we need right now. A little dose of reality, a challenge. Someone to say that the world is ours for the taking if we just believe in ourselves and our abilities. So stop being helpless, begging babies and go out into the world and kick some ass. Stop holding up the very worst of ourselves as culture, as something to revere, to be proud of. We portray ourselves as pimps, hos, and thugs, so why are we surprised when someone characterizes us as such? Lil Wayne and 50 Cent can call our women hos, but Don Imus can't? What sense does that make? Let's stop protesting random slurs and random epithets and random nooses and start marching against our kids dropping out of school, our black men killing each other, and our women exploiting themselves. Would Harriet Tubman want us all standing around waiting on a check? Would Charles Hamilton Houston, who sacrificed his life so we could have equal access to education, want us all dropping out of the schools he fought to desegregate? Sure, there's racism, but those things in our lives we CAN control, we SHOULD control and then excel. No excuses. Fighting injustice and racism is not incompatible with getting a job and acting like you got some damn sense. How about we do both?

See what I mean? It's like that every day. Jam the Negro takes on Jam the American in a battle of the wills. So sue me; that's the reality for so many African Americans today who have been made to feel like heretics for asking for us to be accountable to ourselves first, to our communities first.

I happen to be one of those crazy wack jobs who believes the answer to our problems isn't in a piece of legislation or a law or a check or a new policy. It's within ourselves. Does that make me less black? I'm also tired of the fact that the primary measures of my blackness are whether I agree with Tavis Smiley or attend the Jena Six marches or celebrate Kwanzaa (which, by the way, is some bullshit). And my journey through the black cyberworld has shown me that I am not alone.

There are so many of us who feel this way. We are not the liberal elite; we are not nationalist ex-revolutionaries; we are not trust-fund babies or great scholars. We are simply a broad contingent of men and women who love our communities and want them to flourish. And as quiet as it's kept, there are a lot more of us than you think. Instead of denying the duality as an elitist dilemma of those who really aren't DOWN, we should work together and figure things out and acknowledge that at times we do feel distant from some of our brothers and sisters.

Though I am often conflicted, I refuse to be a slave to the lockstep of the black thought police who march together in a synchronicity not unlike the North Korean army, ready to silence the opposition. If only they'd realize the opposition wants the same thing. The opposition is their biggest champion.

Why can't you be black and act like you have some damn sense without being vilified for challenging others to do the same? Should I just stand by while teenagers disrespect the elderly (and everybody else) on the bus, parents buy kids more clothes than books, and young women go to school looking like they just came from the ho stroll? But if I talk about it publicly and denigrate it on the Internet, I'm a sell-out Uncle Tom exploiting my people.

For example: I get really pissed off when some of my neighbors incessantly throw chicken bones and other trash in front of their homes and have no regard for maintaining the neighborhood. And when my white neighbors mention it, I am embarrassed and uncomfortable and don't quite know what to say. I feel like I can't agree with them without betraying some clandestine Black Chicken Bone Brotherhood and perpetuating the Negro/chicken stereotype.

But on the other hand, why should folks get a pass on littering up the neighborhood just because they are black? Isn't that expecting less? Isn't that insulting? It's like some admission that they really don't know better, and I just don't buy that. Everyone should have pride in where they live and have a responsibility to maintain the neighborhood. So, in the end, I usually punk out and give some vague nod and start talking about my dog's runny bowels.

Frankly, the worst thing I believe we all can do is be silent. If I can't talk to the white guy about the chicken bones strewn about the neighborhood without being some elitist, self-hating Uncle Tom, aren't we all then just doomed to live in a sea of wings and drumstick bones? I know DuBois is probably spinning in his grave at his duality concept being applied to chicken bones and awkward hood conversations, but the bottom line remains the same. Being black can often be fraught with conflict and contradiction. Duality is a bitch. And then you blog.

Being a real, live, thinking black person in the beginning of the 21st century is a hard row to hoe. You can't say anything negative about welfare, Barack Obama, single mothers, Tupac, or affirmative action. If you do you, you may be labeled a sell-out or (gasp) a Republican. But the reality is that we are so much more complicated than these "blackness" litmus tests. There are lots of us who love Jay-Z but hate our country's welfare policies. We may support Barack Obama but are perhaps starting to have doubts about affirmative action and its place in the 21st century. We like Juan Williams and Louis Farrakhan, but Tavis Smiley gets on our nerves and we think Michael Baisden is an idiot.

It's a path filled with conflict and self-doubt, but I think if we ever are to evolve as a community, we must acknowledge the differences and mine them for their value instead of immediately castigating those who think outside of the proverbial box. There are too many knee-jerk, emotional reactions to differences of opinion rather than careful thought and consideration as to how different philosophies borne by different experiences can actually complement one another and act as an agent that unifies us.

Consider the book by Dambisa Moyo. Moyo is a Harvard- and Oxford-educated native of Zambia who wrote a book called *Dead Aid: Why Aid Is Not Working and How There Is a Better Way for Africa.* The book is about her views on many African countries' increasing reliance on aid from the West. Over the years she has seen poverty increase and conditions worsen. She feels many African nations have developed an overreliance on aid, which traps them in a cycle of corruption, dependence, and poverty.

She believes the answer to long-term growth for African nations lies in bond issues, trade, microfinance, and foreign investment. Aid keeps these governments in an eternal position of reliance when the goal should be forming self-sufficient governments. She believes aid to Africa should stop within the next 10 years. She wants the future of African nations to be put back into the hands of African leaders, not in the hands of foreign aid organizations.

Moyo's views have been called controversial, and she has angered many in the Aid-for-Africa community. Even Africa's own honorary native son, Bono, vehemently disagrees. His organization, One, calls it a "poor polemic." My point, and I do have one, is that this is a woman who is clearly a champion for her native continent, who wants to present new ideas and fresh alternatives to the problems of poverty and dependence in Africa. However, her views are so against the paradigm many hold in their heads about Africa and its supplicant role in the world that she is immediately dismissed by some as an off-base wack job. She wants to change the paradigm of dependence and foster self-sufficiency for the continent. But that kind of "radical" perspective seems to threaten those who devoted their lives to either organizing aid or receiving it.

Often views on social issues are so myopic that any challenge to the status quo brings about instant protest. It seems we often have an aversion to looking at problems in a different way. Is there any doubt she wants Africa to thrive? So why not start a meaningful dialogue with her and together create new solutions and proposals and put forth new ideas. Perhaps in the midst of the old and the new, we can forge successful policies. Uganda's Bead for Life program, which focuses on entrepreneurship, can peacefully coexist with Feed the Children. It's not always either/or; sometimes it's both/and.

We are often forced by our communities to be this or that. While it was a very entertaining song by Black Sheep when I was in college, it is in no way a productive strategy for advancing the race. For so long, you had to be DuBois or Booker T., Malcolm or Martin, a revolutionary or an Uncle Tom, a thug or an oreo. There is so much gray area between these extremes that we never explore. And the irony is that most black folks exist in this gray area.

We must stop limiting ourselves to the this-or-that mentality and start exploring all the exciting thoughts and ideas of that gray area in between. Our history has produced some of the most dynamic thinkers and personalities the world has ever seen. Yet some of them are dismissed summarily simply because they have the "wrong" political affiliation, the "wrong" accent, or the "wrong" color spouse. If Barack Obama, who has the potential to be one of the greatest presidents of this nation, had a white wife, is there any doubt he would have been defeated early on in the race? While you may not agree with every aspect of a person's life, he or she may also have ideas you support or that are beneficial to your community.

Everything isn't this or that. Sometime it's both; sometimes it's neither. Are we to believe that black conservatives don't care about black people? Or that all black Democrats are working tirelessly for the betterment of the community? We must stop prejudging the value of ideas based on political party, perm or natural, spouse color, or radio station choice. And we can't do that if we're making rash assumptions and wild accusations, jumping to conclusions, and simply not listening.

I've heard my brethren (other black people) instantly dismiss someone's ideas once they learn he/she is a Republican. RUFKM (r u fucking kidding me)? I've seen adults wholly discounted because they classified themselves as biracial or were members of the Heritage Foundation or because they were in Jack and Jill of America or had a white wife or lived in the projects or had a child whose age betrayed the fact that they had been teenage moms. A lockstep of thought, policy, belief, and experience should not be the sine qua non of black progress. Right now, we need anyone who wants our communities to succeed to be a part of the conversation. I don't care how many baby daddies you may have, if you're trying to do the right thing by our communities and the next generation, then you will always be welcome at my table (just don't bring your badass kids).

I also understand that some people have a beef with me not because of what I say but because of how I say it. They would feel much more comfortable if I used the Internet to showcase inspirational poetry, positive images, Black History Month, and interpretive dance. They would love it if my site was a never-ending loop alternating between the "I have a dream" speech and the Rosa Parks story (as narrated by Cicely Tyson). Naaaah.

Sure, my site can be cruel. It's supposed to be; the site is a tool of shame. Somehow along the way we lost shame as a concept. *New York Times* columnist David Brooks once said, albeit in a different context, "Capitalist institutions have to be surrounded by social understandings, by a set of norms that we all adhere to or that are enforced by shame." I believe Brooks is right. There was a time when shame kept young women from getting pregnant, when shame kept unmarried couples from living together, when shame kept you from acting a fool in public because it might get back to your family, when shame kept many off the government dole. Shame is grossly underestimated as a tool for behavior modification.

Unfortunately the concept of shame has been replaced by an "anything goes/if it feels good do it/getting over" mentality. So many of our images and so much of our behavior are just accepted without community scrutiny or any concept of moral standards; I wanted to provide one forum that looked at this stuff and said out loud: **this is unacceptable**. I am that wagging finger that says, "You are not going to behave that way, and you are not leaving the house like that." Because it seems that too many parents, schools, churches, communities, and nonprofits simply refuse to say it. (They may hurt someone's feelings.)

I'm tired of the bullshit, begging, and excuses. Too many people are waiting on a check, and it's making a mockery of what our parents and grandparents died for—and I'll be damned if I'm gonna let the PC Nazis prevent me from speaking out on it. That's real. Speaking out is my way of expressing and coping with that frustration. I figure it's better than Jack Daniels.

The truth is that, for better or worse, the entire community is still most often judged by the actions of a few. That's why we all still look at the evening news and hope that the perpetrator of the latest sensational crime isn't black. We are constantly battling stereotypes, but too many of us choose to embrace those stereotypes as our "culture" and run with them. Am I a bad black person for saying "stop that"?

These are not new or revolutionary concerns; we talk about them in private all the time. And the reason we fill constrained-to-private conversations with such issues is because of the conflict we feel within. How can we uplift black people and acknowledge our faults at the same time? Easy. It's like your parents (or, these days, parent): they can tell you what a wonderful, attractive, intelligent child you are, but at the same time, they don't hesitate to read you the riot act when you act up. It doesn't mean they don't love you; it means they want you to be your best and won't settle for less. I'm like the mean mama of the Internet.

I don't care if you don't like my tactics or if you think I'm mean. But if you listen to what I have to say, then maybe, just maybe, you'll find value there; maybe you'll learn something. A broadening of the discourse can only help the dialogue. Though you may not want to believe it, there are so many dynamic men and women who feel the same way I do. I am not some fringe lunatic who puts out wacky newsletters with misspellings and holds meetings at abandoned storefronts after dark. I am a vibrant, urban woman and more "typical" than you would like to believe. In my social circles, the conversation is more often about black folks getting their shit together than it is about racial oppression. We've moved on from assuming our coworker got fired because she was black to knowing it was only a matter of time before she got fired because her black ass was late every day. Face it: we're here, we jeer—get used to it. What we need now is more thought and more conversation, not less. Pretending that people like me don't exist, that we are some radical fringe element of black life, is outrageous.

Is it great for our community's image if Cosby comes out and calls black folks out for behaving badly? Not really. But does it have value? Yes. Like hotghettomess.com, it starts an important conversation that is long overdue in our communities, our schools, our churches, and our families. It forces us, instead of looking to the White House, to look at our own houses and look at one another to see what responsibility we have for our current condition and what we can do to begin to move in the right direction.

In the end, duality not withstanding, please know that I, along with countless others that I correspond with every day, want only the best for our brothers and sisters. You may not like what I'm saying, but it doesn't mean that it isn't true. Let's stop this tunnel-vision view of what a black person is and how he or she should think and what he or she should say. I can fight for what's best for our communities without having a natural, wearing a ring in my nose, burning incense, dousing myself with fragrant African oil, and downloading the Last Poets onto my iPod. All of our diverse views are necessary if we are ever to craft a comprehensive plan to address some of the most threatening ills in our cities.

I admit my tactics are extreme, but that's how I choose to approach the challenge. I'm bringing shame (as opposed to sexy) back. And frankly, the conversation has not been the same since.

For those who think I speak my mind for the money and criticize me for "making millions off the exploitation of my people" (actual excerpt from an e-mail), the truth is that I'm drowning in debt, haven't bought new clothes in a couple of years, buy my sunglasses from Target, and ask all my friends who work at office jobs to steal reams of paper for my printer. Newsflash: I take all the abuse and criticism and threats of eternal damnation simply because I believe in what I'm doing. I know it's a new concept, but work with me.

I am nothing more than a product of the Negro duality. I was given the opportunity to strive for excellence academically and professionally, and I've taken full advantage, but I also live as a minority—discounted and marginalized and misunderstood with a love and loyalty to my black community. Can't we learn from people like me? This new generation of hybrid, conflicted blacks? We maintain and immerse ourselves in our history, cultural traditions, and pride, but find it very hard to relate to the dysfunction among some black folks that exists today, are disgusted by what often passes for "black culture" these days, and are totally stumped as to why so many blacks have turned their backs on the very opportunities our ancestors have fought for.

We all are accountable. Whether you are out in the world representing black folks badly and acting a fool or you're someone who has never given a dime or an hour to help those less fortunate than yourself, it's all on us. And if we are ever to progress, we must accept the fact that we all don't vote Democratic, some of us have never seen a Tyler Perry movie (let alone a stage play), we don't all listen to Tom Joyner or the *Steve Harvey Morning Show,* and there are many who think that Bill Cosby was 100 percent right. Some of us don't watch *House of Payne* and would never pay any amount of money to see Diddy on Broadway. This doesn't mean we're damaged, confused black goods and must be moles for The Man. It's this approach to defining blackness that often marginalizes the very members of the community that could help us most. Remember when black folks were asking themselves if Obama was black enough (whatever that means)? Lunacy.

We should embrace the diversity of our existence as blacks in America. We should build on that coalition of different experiences, beliefs, perspectives, and philosophies. We all won't think alike (thank God). We all won't agree. But that is what America is about. Our ancestors fought and died to become part of this great democracy, yet within our own communities we undermine their achievements by silencing or ignoring or demonizing those whose views may be different than ours, those who don't fit into our preconceived notion of what a "real" black person is.

Some do have very different views of race in the world today and our current role in society. Does that make them less black? Less vested in our success? Of course not. It just means that I, and many others in my generation, have grown up with a new vantage point on race, one where we feel as though we are straddling two worlds, one of racial loyalty, and one of American ideals and opportunity. Sometimes the two coexist peacefully and sometimes they don't. Which makes it hard to plan the day.

2

C IS FOR CRAP:
STANDARDS,
SCHMANDARDS

"I was raised to believe that excellence is the best deterrent to racism or sexism, and that's how I operate my life."
—Oprah Winfrey

If you pay attention to black popular culture, you'll find a lot of talk about bars. People meet at the bar, they sip Patrón at the bar, and (as T-Pain reminds us in his hit song) occasionally they fall in love with the bartender. Hotghettomess.com was created to bring back into the conversation a bar we don't talk about much anymore. The proverbial bar of standards.

At one time, that bar of standards acted as a moral compass. It guided us through our daily lives and challenged us to always be on our best behavior. It was the bar that made you think twice before engaging in certain activities because you knew it would disgrace your family. It was the bar that created the sense of paranoia that someone was always watching who would tell your mama on you. As of now, the bar of morality is so low that even that roller-skating kid from India could not limbo under it.

Now, I want to get something straight early on. I am no one's moral guide, trust. With the number of skeletons in my closet, I in no way have the authority to set the bar for behavior. But when I was growing up, at least there WAS a bar. Believe me, I KNEW when I was fucking up. And those values that were instilled in me as a child created a foundation so I never veered too far off track. When I did wrong, at least I knew it. What I don't understand about life in many urban communities today is that the bar of expectations and standards has been crushed up and discarded like an empty pack of Newports (soft pack, not the box).

The initial philosophy behind hotghettomess.com was a reexamination of community values and standards of behavior. (And you thought it was just a site full of dumb-ass pictures.) If the pictures I was seeing permeate the Internet were any indication of what was appropriate behavior in our communities, particularly by young people, then Jesus needed to be called. Quick. And what I find even stranger than the wild, rampant acting out of young people, which is really nothing new, is the total willful ignorance that the rest of the community seems to be engaged in. How could a generation stray so far off course and the community remain silent?

I found it odd that we will march enthusiastically and threaten boycotts and demand that others be held accountable for offenses against the black community, yet, when it comes to the behaviors of our own, like black-on-black crime or high drop-out rates, we look the other way. Shouldn't we be just as vigilant (and some might argue more vigilant) when it comes to demanding the accountability of one another? The destructive behavior so many of us are engaging in does more damage to communities than any random noose or racial slur ever could.

Sooooo, since families and neighborhoods and teachers and churches and mainstream media personalities don't talk about it, I do.

Let's be clear, the decline of standards and morality is certainly not specific to the black community. America in general has pretty much lost its damn mind. But nowhere have the effects of a general lack of mores been as drastic and as devastating as among the African American community. When we look at out-of-wedlock births, juvenile crime, HIV infection, the high school drop-out rate, the number of black men in jail—and the list goes on and on—it's easy to see why we should be very concerned. But what all the statistics don't reflect is the apathy I sense from members of my community. Which, on some level, is even more frightening.

Where is the concern? Where is the outrage? Gone is the concern for our collective progress. There is no "our" anymore. There is "me," "mine," and "them." Our communities have been reduced to "anything goes" parties. It's like our lives are daily raves where if it feels good, we do it. And it's killing us. We eat, drink, spend, and have reckless sex with reckless abandon. As a result we're too fat, too dumb, too broke, and have too many kids out of wedlock.

Our collective notion of what is right and wrong and good and bad for our communities has turned into a hodgepodge of nihilistic, libertarian, and hedonistic philosophies, all converging on street corners, neighborhoods, and the minds of our young people. A community without societal standards and mores is like a child without discipline, wild and out of control. And no one wants to be bothered by him.

What are we so afraid of? Why don't we tell our young women that dressing with their titties and asses hanging out is unacceptable? Why can't we tell our young men that dressing so that everyone can see their whole pair of drawers will not be tolerated? There was a time when parents were not the only enforcers of standards, when the community at large had implied permission to enforce them as well.

For example, when I see a young woman going to the prom looking like a streetwalker, I'm always saddened to think about the sheer number of people who have failed her. Clearly, her parents are, or parent is, deficient in judgment for allowing this young woman to be dressed so inappropriately. But then where are our community safety nets? If the parent is an idiot, then the chaperones, administrators, and principal at that school should take a stand and say to that young lady, "You will not come here dressed that way."

Those outrageous and often X-rated prom pictures were the cata-lyst for my newfound activism. It was shocking that communities were not only willing to allow their young women to present themselves this way, but also that they were complicit. Often the offending dresses were made by the mother.

I was thrilled to finally see some news reports last year about prin-cipals who refused entry to prom to teenagers who were dressed inap-propriately. Thank God someone finally stood up and said enough is enough. And you know the parents probably read those principals the riot act about their kids being denied entrance. But who cares; it was absolutely the right thing to do. If they want to dress like hookers, they can take their fast tails somewhere else. If only more adults in our com-munities and schools had the balls to challenge this behavior, to let their daughters know, "You will not walk out of my house looking like that." Kudos to organizations like the National Council of Negro Women, the Boys and Girls Clubs of America, Girls Inc., Girl Scouts of America, and the many African American sororities for encouraging women to focus on education, strive for excellence, serve their communities, and conduct themselves like ladies. We simply can't afford to encourage a generation to be nothing more than walking tits and asses. They are far too valuable for that. We owe them so much more than that.

Now, inappropriate dressing is an extreme example of our reluc-tance to enforce standards, but there are smaller, more prevalent exam-ples in our communities. I often talk about my grammar pet peeves, and it's not just because I'm trying to be obnoxious. It's about playing the game, people. Our grammar and way of speaking can often shut doors of opportunity for us before we walk in the room. Much like your appearance, your way of speaking says a lot about you. Is it fair that you are judged on how you speak? No. But life isn't fair. In the real world, nothing says *dumb* like a bunch of improper English. Now hear me out.

I am in no way saying that you should never use bad English, colloquialisms, profanity, and slang. There is just a time and place for it. Believe me, I use bad English all the time and can cuss like a Southern sailor. But I know the appropriate times to do so and can switch it off in a New York minute if need be. And therein lies the problem. Many of our young people do not know the difference.

As adults we must teach them how to survive in this world. They must learn that there is a difference between how you speak on the corner and how you speak in an interview or in a classroom or in the workplace. My parents corrected me nonstop. It is up to us to give young people everything they need to be successful. Sometimes that means listening and correcting and enforcing to them that the corporate world may not be appreciative of their colorful vernacular.

In a world where we are judged by employers in the first five minutes, we must give our children the tools to succeed. Something as small as requiring them to speak correctly sends the signal that there is a difference between hip-hop life and real life. Many of them just don't know. As a teacher of college students, I was really shocked at the way young people expressed themselves in the classroom. Who told them this was acceptable? Why do they think this is OK? This may be fine on their demo tape or on their Facebook pages but not the real world. I'm sure even President Obama can spout some serious F-bombs now and then (especially with this economy), but he knows there is a time and place.

I love my people and our creative use of the English language, but if we love our young people, we must teach them how to navigate this complex world and how to turn their hip-hop alter egos on and off. They can't speak the same way 50 Cent does when they go interview for their summer job.

We must teach them that even in the Age of Obama, they have to be twice as good, twice as smart, and twice as focused. It's about knowing where you are and what is appropriate. They can act a fool at home or at play, but when it comes down to business and education, the standards are different, and they need to know how to rise to the occasion. Only we can teach them that.

From dress to grammar and everything in between, we must raise our expectations and encourage high standards of behavior from everyone in our neighborhoods. There is so much we can learn from our history in this country. We must realize that success as a community has less to do with stuff than with values. I look at the generations before me, who had less stuff but more integrity, more dignity, more pride, and more hope. For example, according to the United States Census, the median income of an African American family in 1964 was $18,859. Today, that median income has risen to over $30,000. But along with our increase in income has come a decline in cultural values, intact families, and the sense of a common goal. We make more money, yet, in too many communities, our children are killing each other in the streets, parents are abandoning their children, and kids are dropping out of high school. So is it really about money—or is it about us?

So many would have us believe that if you are poor, then you simply face unavoidable pathos, and there's not much that can be done about it. We have adopted this mentality and accepted destructive behaviors as part of some inevitable culture of poverty. This only breeds a generation that uses its current station in life as a perpetual excuse not to do the best they can. And when we don't expect it from them, why should they perform? As motivational speaker Les Brown said, "No one rises to low expectations."

Can you imagine if prior generations just threw up their hands and said, *Well, we're poor, so what's the point of hard work or education? I'm broke and everyone I know is broke, so fuck it.* Fortunately for all of us, they didn't do that. They worked and strived and dreamed. Although times were tough, they saw an opportunity for their children to do better than they did. They knew education and hard work were the key. Success wasn't just going to fall in their laps, but it was indeed possible.

Throughout our history we were expected to do well by an entire community. Regardless of economic status, whole communities rallied around children to get them through high school and college. Neighbors watched out for neighbors, and teachers were the bosses of the classrooms. The value of education was ever present and hung over you like a specter.

There was an understanding of what our ancestors had gone through just to survive in American society, and it was unthinkable to piss that up. Though times were hard, there was also a sense of opportunity, and possibility, and everyone around you was going to make sure you took full advantage.

You were expected to behave and conduct yourself in a way that would not shame your family, in a way that would make your mama proud. The moral compass was functioning, and although maybe you got off course every now and then, there was generally someone with a side-eye and an ass-whuppin' to make sure you didn't stray too far.

Much like Steve Fossett, those expectations have disappeared. One day I looked up and it was suddenly the pinnacle of achievement for a black male to finish high school. NO, you're SUPPOSED to finish high school. College and even graduate school should be a default. Now it's a badge of honor if some man is actually taking care of his children. NO, you're SUPPOSED to.

It seems like the last 20 years have brought, along with YouTube and a black president, a drastic drop in expectations. Not only have these lower expectations produced a generation of apathetic, mandarin-minded boys and girls, they have also set up a generation to be the willing players of the underclass. And we should be ashamed of ourselves.

Just when did we turn from a community who believed that anything was possible with hard work to a community who is working on our GED? Fifty years after the *Brown v. Board* decision, with a record amount of funding for schools, we still have many inner cities with only half of black students graduating from high school. Is more money REALLY the answer?

I was taught early on that I could be anything I wanted to be. My destiny was limitless, and Cs were unacceptable. I never realized how valuable a lesson it was until one day I looked around at youth who had no vision. Mediocrity and apathy run rampant. Young people's vision often goes no farther than what they'll be wearing next week. There is no sense of the bigness of the world or the unlimited potential for their lives.

❏ **Mediocrity is your enemy.**

❏ **Strive for excellence in everything you do and encourage your children and others in your life to do the same.**

It's ironic that in an age where so much information has become available to us and opportunities abound, we seem more myopic and visionless than ever. It defies logic that as the world opens up to us, we close to it, more comfortable with the faux security of a hard swagger and a cool pose and a bad ARM loan. It feels like we're in this perpetual state of getting by. We're not even scratchin' and surviving anymore, we're just surviving—and this lack of passion for not only our communities but also, to a greater degree, our own lives has created a generation that defines itself by the mundane. And it's even more frightening that no one is challenging it—hell, no one is even acknowledging it.

In a world where the economy is global and the signals are digital, it is the time to challenge our young people to do better than before. Our standards must be higher, our expectations greater, or we will not be able to take advantage of the opportunities afforded us by the sacrifices of our ancestors.

And there seems to be a misconception that this lack of standards and lowering of expectations are only low-income/public-school/inner-city issues. Nothing could be further from the truth. Communities across the socioeconomic and geographic spectrum are wrestling with young people who no longer can see beyond the next model of their cell phone and parents who are just too tired and stressed out to really give two shits. As our lives get busier, the enthusiastic focus on our children's education is replaced by overtime at work, a social life, or the rigors of having to do double duty as mom and dad.

JAM THE NEGRO

Here we go again with this apathy nonsense being spewed by some arugula-eating, elitist liberal who claims she's just interested in helping. Well, no thanks, sweetie. How dare you talk about mediocrity and high standards? Don't you know it's all a lot of us can do just to survive the day? You clearly lead a life in which you don't have to struggle. You can sit back and pontificate on a bunch of bullshit that everybody else needs to be doing. Who are you to tell me what my standards should be? Not all of us are out here on the corner. There are folks who make an honest living, who are trying to navigate a world where all the cards are stacked against us. And instead of offering a helping hand, you and your kind just sit there and tell everyone what they're doing wrong. Have you ever thought of writing about what we're doing *right*? Damn. We should enforce standards? We try to do that, but it's really hard to compete with the images that are being fed to our children by hip-hop and cable. Why don't you take your complaints where it counts? To the real forces of power. The media. They are the ones who are inundating our young people with negative imagery and making them think that black culture is all about how far your pants are hanging off your ass. Yeah, but you let them off the hook. You want to go after young, impressionable teenagers who don't know shit from shinola. You conservative types are always blaming the victim. The mainstream media is what's really dooming our kids. I can enforce all the standards I want, but if they want to look like the young girls in the videos, what am I supposed to do? It's just a different time. Everyone doesn't still live in the '60s. Why don't you adjust your argument to the 21st century and then maybe we can talk. If you are poor, then you generally don't have a chance in this country no matter what color you are. That's just real talk.

JAM THE AMERICAN

Yes, you may be struggling. Yes, the cards are stacked against you and played from the bottom of the deck. And? So you get a pass to be less than your best? Doesn't coming from a place of disadvantage mean you have to be even better? My parents always told me that because I was black I had to be twice as good. Should our expectations of each other be based on socioeconomic status? Or does everyone have a responsibility to those who came before us to be his or her best and expect the best from others? Maybe you got the short end of the stick, or maybe you made a bunch of bad decisions. Either way you don't get an "It's OK to be mediocre" card—we just can't afford it. This world is increasingly about results and what value you bring to the table. You can't come to the table value-less and then complain that all you get is scraps. Of course the media is hard to contend with, but there's a simple answer: cut the goddamned TV off for a change. It kills me how black folks complain about the negative imagery in the media, yet they allow their kids to be glued to BET 24 hours a day and drop them off to every gangsta movie ever made. And God forbid something positive or educational comes out—no one even supports it. How can we ask studios to make more positive films and TV shows when we don't support the positive projects that do come out? Can you say *Akeelah and the Bee?* We are so full of shit sometimes. Either way, media should not be raising your kids. We should demand nothing but excellence regardless of external circumstances. If you raise children expecting the best, then they will learn that the best is the standard by which they will be judged. Can you imagine a community where all of our children strive to be the best? So stop complaining, turn off the TV, check some homework, and demand more from your kids—and everyone else's kids, too.

Now, I'm not Mary Poppins. I know firsthand that even in the best situations a promising young person can often still fall victim to "just doing enough." Case in point: my neighbor. He's bright, handsome, and sweet, but unfortunately he is on his way to becoming depressingly average.

Let me explain. My neighbor grew up in a working-class suburb. He was surrounded by a family who loved him; he was an average student, part of a sports team, and an all-around good kid. He got into college on an athletic scholarship, and I could not have been prouder. Although he had close family members that pursued higher education, his mom, dad, and grandmother never went to college, so it was a great achievement for him to be attending a local university on scholarship. I was thrilled that, growing up in an area where very few black men go on to pursue higher education, he seemed to be on the right path to better himself and, most important, act as an example to his two younger brothers.

But things didn't go quite as planned. In the summer before his junior year, I got the news from my mom that my neighbor wasn't going back to college. I immediately called him to ask what the deal was. He told me that he had lost his scholarship (his story changed several times as to exactly why this happened) and he could no longer afford to attend the school. He was going to work for the next semester, save money, and go back to school in the spring or the following year.

Well, we all know what that means. Most folks who leave college never go back, and I was determined that he get his college degree. So I offered to pay his tuition. I didn't care what I had to do—whether it was taking out loans or selling ass on 12th Street, I was making sure that boy graduated from college.

See, I am blessed to have come from a family where education was stressed, Cs were not acceptable, and college was not optional. So I tried to convince him of the importance of his staying in school and getting his college degree. And even with my offer to pay his entire tuition, he refused. He wanted to work, and by working he could save for school and also get a car. After I tried and tried to persuade him, it became clear to me that his desire for a car was far stronger than his desire to get a college degree.

So, long story short (I know, too late), he ends up working at some dead-end, random job, he never goes back to college, and now has three kids by three different women. He's not even 24. I feel like somehow I failed him; his family—my family—failed him. I know there is nothing we could have physically done, but I can't shake the feeling that our family, our community, let a vibrant life full of potential slowly descend into mediocrity—and never said a word. Maybe never even noticed.

I keep looking back at what I could have done, what I could have said to change his path. But how do you convince a young man to finish college when he's been raised in a world that tells him he should be happy just getting out of high school? My voice was lost among his friends and teachers and media who told him that good enough was enough. Those who told him that passing is passing, even if it's with a D.

> ❑ **C stands for "crap." Adopt the outlook that a C is never acceptable.**
>
> ❑ **The possibilities for your children's lives are endless, and you must tell them that every day.**

And what was most frustrating is that I couldn't write it off as someone who didn't know any better. He has college graduates and successful people around him, and if you ask him, he knows he should have stayed. He knows the decision was an incorrect one. However, it STILL didn't matter. This is what scares me about our young people; there is an alarming amount of complacency, lack of vision, and zest for life. There are so many young people like my neighbor out there. People who have been exposed to opportunity, whose parents cared and pushed and tried. Some of those very kids are voluntarily chucking education, succumbing to the will of the streets, and embracing the lure of parties and bullshit. And if *these* kids blow off opportunity, what hope is there for those who face the challenges of poverty, crime, and uninvolved parents?

Me and my smart mouth were no match against "easy," against "quick," against "right now." My neighbor is a great kid, and it hurts my soul whenever I see potential squandered. Especially when someone is handing you an opportunity on a platter. I mean, if you're not willing to accept an opportunity when someone is GIVING it to you, what happens if one day you actually have to work for it? I don't know. Maybe that's the problem—we've been giving too much and expecting too little.

See, for too long we have defined failure by its extreme manifes-tations: ending up in jail, becoming a drug addict, being a teenage mother. But, in my opinion, when we don't see a young person all the way through to realizing his or her potential, it's just as big a failure. In our community, mediocrity is becoming an epidemic. And that realiza-tion hit me really close to home. I wonder what will become of these young people? In a world and an economy where there is little use for the ordinary, what happens to this generation?

Where are the dreamers? Who are the innovators? Where are the parents who don't allow failure, who read to their children, who tell them in the dark of night as they put them to bed: "You can be anything you want to in this world, and the possibilities for your life are endless"?

Our bar of standards has dropped so low that as long as teenag-ers graduate from high school, we say they're doing fine. As long as they aren't in the system, we say they're doing fine. Yes, maybe they are doing fine, but true excellence is scarce. Vision is nonexistent. You have a 62-inch flat screen, and your kid doesn't have a computer in the home. We aren't taking foreign languages; we aren't going into technol-ogy fields.

We should harken back to the mentality of our predecessors and embrace a philosophy of goals and success and striving to be the best and reaching the highest of heights. The *New York Times* reported in 1996 that between 1880 and 1910 the percentage of black people who could read and write went from 30 to 70. This is despite an environment that openly brutalized black Americans, where racism was overt, intim-idation common, and schoolhouses were often the center of racially charged violence. Now I'm sorry—what's your excuse again?

In this global economy, we cannot afford average. This is no longer a world where you can graduate from high school, join a union, and work in a factory for 30 years and still be able to raise a family. By not challenging each other to be the best in whatever we do, we are doing ourselves a disservice and, more important, we are setting our young people up to be members of a self-imposed underclass. Our high school graduation rates have not changed significantly in the last 25 years, even though this has been a time of great economic and educational strides for many black households. When will we learn that money is often not the issue?

With access to more opportunities than ever, our young people seem perfectly content settling for less. And although I lay this issue out in very simplistic terms, it is actually an extremely complex problem to tackle. I didn't realize what a fine line you have to walk in order to encourage and support young people but at the same time not accept less from them—until I became a college professor. And I have to admit, there were many times when I simply didn't know what to do with them. I realized that my experience was a microcosm of what parents and other educators nationwide often face.

Yes, people actually entrusted me with the minds of college students. Scary, I know. But this is what struck me: students at my college were clearly products of a public education system that had failed many of them. They would turn in assignments that were generally on the ninth- and tenth-grade level. If I were to grade their papers objectively, 90 percent of my students would have received Ds or Fs.

So I had to figure out what sort of teacher I wanted to be. I had to figure out how to enforce high standards among students who didn't know what a high standard was. Do I fail everyone? Will that teach them to step up their game? Maybe. Or they'll just drop the class. College should be about expanding the mind. It should be about critical thinking, analysis, broadening your worldview, and developing your global perspective, not learning when and when not to capitalize. There had to be another way that wouldn't destroy their GPAs but at the same time wouldn't amount to the collegiate version of social promotion.

I kept asking myself how students could graduate from high school and get through two or three years of college and not have basic language and writing skills. Though I'm not a writing teacher and mine was not an English class, I just couldn't let this go. Most importantly, I couldn't let these students go into the real, globalized world and not be prepared. But I felt that so much of their substandard academic performance was simply because, along the way, no one cared enough to challenge them to do any better.

So I tried to assess students primarily on critical-thinking skills while providing in-depth feedback on their writing. I was very honest about the deficiencies in their work. Sometimes it would take a whole page to outline my notes and suggestions on their writing. And while they by no means turned into John Updikes and Toni Morrisons, they did improve, and, best of all, they now knew they had to do better. They knew that what they were doing was not good enough. I certainly couldn't solve all the problems brought on by their lifetime of substandard education in one semester, but I could let them know that where they were was not good enough. What they were doing was not good enough. It was unacceptable in the real world. I was nurturing and encouraging, but in the end it was imperative that they do better.

Some students responded; some didn't. Some students got it; others were clearly doomed to be idiots. What can you do?

Maybe I should have failed them and told them that their writing was unacceptable at this level. Isn't that what their bosses would tell them? I didn't want to treat these young adults like babies, just telling them what they wanted to hear and shuffling them off to the next level. But they didn't deserve to fail. The public education system clearly failed them. I'm still conflicted to this day. Did I mention that none of this was easy?

Our job as teachers, neighbors, and parents is to say, "You can do better." Don't get me wrong: we also must tell them how great they are and what unlimited potential they have. But we MUST challenge our young people to excel. I wonder how many of these students' teachers just gave them a B or a C and then hurried home to catch *Grey's Anatomy*.

And I can't help but think that it's our fault. Have we told them that there's more, have we shown them what more looks like? Have we reinforced in them every waking moment that they can dream big and achieve their goals through education and hard work?

Young people need something by which to measure their achievement. We have to reinforce that THINGS are not achievements. They need goals. Lofty goals. Their intellect should be constantly challenged. Mediocrity should never be acceptable.

Ultimately, it's not what material treasure we provide our children; treasure can be squandered and wasted. Only in instilling a largeness of vision can we sustain them through the good and the bad decisions they will make along the way. When you have vision, you can see your potential. You

- ❏ Doing just enough to get by should not be your life philosophy.
- ❏ Whatever you do, take pride in it and excel (even if you hate it). Excellence opens doors.
- ❏ "Good enough" is never good enough.

know the world holds no limits for you. Without vision, you become short-sighted, and when you are short-sighted you often make bad decisions that will no doubt affect your long-term goals. Even as adults, as we go through our daily lives, it is time we extend our perspective from what's easy and start raising the bar for ourselves. Don't coast; excel.

Children learn what they live, and our lives should all be lived to the absolute fullest, with the quest for excellence being the rule, not the exception. Challenge yourselves, your children, and your community as a whole to raise the bar in their lives. You should expect the best always, and you should decry any form of settling in those around you.

As the saying goes, "You only rise to the level of what is expected of you." We have dropped the ball and lowered expectations for too long. No one has bothered to say, "We expect more of our young men and women." No one says, "In our community, this is unacceptable." No one has marched; no one has protested the state of our young people and our families.

It's time we expect more of ourselves and each other and not be afraid to speak out against actions or behaviors that are below the standards we set for our community. It's time to recapture our vision and dream big. Let's get rid of this "getting by" mentality. As my dad once told me when I brought home a subpar report card, "C is for 'crap.'"

I love my community, and it's the people we love that we should be hardest on. Why do you think I'm so hard on black folks? It just frustrates me when it seems the only thing standing in the way of our self-actualization as a community is ourselves.

3

THEY DON'T
KNOW ANY
BETTER?

"Truth knows no color, it appeals to intelligence."
—Ralph Wiley

You know, I have been cussed out, yelled at, condemned to hell, and rebuked in the name of Jesus by a variety of people for speaking my mind on the state of the black community. However, the feedback I get is overwhelmingly positive, so I don't stress too much about the folks who call me a race traitor, an elitist, a self-righteous bitch, or a member of the GOP. But one conversation I had recently, although I had heard it a million times before, really got me thinking.

One afternoon I decided to live on the edge a bit and answer the little blue phone that is my business line. Turns out it was a gentleman calling me after finding out that one of his friends (I suspect it was his girlfriend) had the dubious distinction of being called a hot ghetto mess on my Web site. So I spoke to him and patiently listened as he told me what a horrible, ugly, mean person I am.

So as I try to divide my attention between his tirade and cleaning the little, hard doo-doo balls out of my dog's ass, something he said struck me as it never had before. He said that although he understood my intent, what I was doing was mean-spirited because black people "just don't know any better."

Now, granted, I've heard this a million times before, and that sentiment has become so cliché that I never really pay any attention to it, but for some reason those words on that day stood out to me like a virgin at a prison rodeo. And it caused me to wonder . . .

At this point in the game, do people really not know any better?

I feel like the only people who can really claim not to know any better are children, Patty Hearst (and I'm STILL not convinced), or feral people like Nell in that movie. The assertion that somehow, today, grown-ass people don't know any better is ridiculous. And it's not only ridiculous, it's also a dangerous, dismissive, and paternalistic way to regard members of our community. It immediately removes from people all responsibility for their actions.

Yet we seem very comfortable about using this phrase with regard to black folks' behavioral issues. I hear this justification used to excuse everyone—criminals, bad parents, *Maury* show guests, drug dealers, bad teachers, and hip-hop artists. Odds are, if someone has embarrassed the black race somewhere, someone else will confidently explain that she or he just didn't know any better. Frankly, the criticism I hear most often (other than that I'm a self-righteous, money-grubbin' bitch) is "You're making fun of poor people who don't know any better." Let me straighten this out once and for all.

❑ **Unless you are a feral child or are mentally challenged, you DO know better.**

First, I don't make fun of poor people. Perhaps if I were down in Appalachia or on the Mississippi Delta or down in Haiti snapping photos and cracking jokes, then your beef may be justified. However, if fools have the money to go clubbing, pop bottles of Moët, and buy a horrific outfit every week solely for the occasion, then they are far from poor and garner none of my sympathy. If you can have a diamond-encrusted DVD belt that plays actual movies, or a tattoo that says #1 DICK SUCKA on your chest, then you are not broke (those tats are expensive) and are ripe for ridicule. Got it?

> ❑ Socioeconomic status does not dictate what behavior should be expected or accepted. All people should be expected to act with dignity and respect for themselves and others at all times.

However, let's assume *arguendo* that one is poor. Let's say you were not dealt a particularly good hand in life, and you struggle financially. You are poor, your mama was poor, and your grandmama was poor. What exactly does that mean in terms of what should be expected of you? Does being of modest means give you a free pass in terms of standards of behavior and expectations? Or should you be expected to conduct yourself in an appropriate manner regardless of tax bracket?

Unfortunately, we have begun to delineate what is and isn't appropriate behavior based on socioeconomic status. There is no one standard of behavior that everyone is expected to live up to. Expectations seem to differ depending on the zip code. It is the reason that teachers in low-income schools expect less from their students; it's why no one bothers to pick up trash in front of his or her home in certain neighborhoods; it's why horrific violence in certain areas rarely makes the front page, and everyone just stands around and watches. As a community we have bought into the idea of lowering our expectations based on income and neighborhood.

Values are not malleable; they don't shape-shift depending on who you are and what your background is. That's why it's called a community—because we are all in this together. As such, we all must be accountable for our behavior and hold everyone responsible for the whole community's welfare. We can't have a different code of ethics for one side of town.

That being said, I am also sick of hearing people blame bad decisions, bad behavior, and bad kids on the hood. The hood is not a license to ill.

I have a huge problem with the lack of money being equated with the lack of morals and, most important, the lack of accountability. I also have an even huger (is that a word?) problem with the backlash you face if you ever voice this sentiment above a whisper in public. When did it become such a sin against humanity to suggest that people get it together and not behave in a way that is detrimental to themselves, their children, and their community? When was it classified a felony to speak out against bad behavior?

So am I supposed to be fine with kids on the bus in the morning loudly cursing and disrespecting everyone within the sound of their voice because their moms make minimum wage or are on public assistance? Am I supposed to excuse a student assaulting his or her teacher because he or she comes from a single-parent home? Am I cool with a man who doesn't support his children because his dad wasn't around? Of course not—no matter what your economic status, you should be expected to act with respect, class, and dignity at all times. You should raise and support the children you produce, and you should work to better the lives of your offspring. You should be expected to be a productive member of society, no matter what circumstances you came from. Period. Nothing less is acceptable.

Of course, the playing field is not level. Life is absolutely much harder on some than it is on others. But that means we, as a community, should step in and work to be the safety nets for those people, not write off dysfunctional behavior as inevitable. We can't feel guilty about demanding more simply because someone may have certain disadvantages. Demanding more could be the very thing that saves a person from repeating the mistakes of the past. Knowing that there is more, that we expect more, and that someone is capable of doing more is invaluable.

I remember growing up I had a neighbor who made it his business to let my mom know if I had boys in the house while she was gone, if I stole the car, or if I snuck out of the house late at night. Of course, back then, I hated him with a passion like no other. I remember plotting one day, after he snitched on me, to throw a big rock through the window of his brand-new silver Corvette. I just couldn't quite muster up the balls to do it.

My neighbor understood that my behavior was unacceptable, and he was not going to just stand by and watch me engage in acts that could possibly derail my life and all the hopes and dreams my parents had for me. It was because he cared that he told my parents about my chicanery. It wasn't about minding his own business or not snitching or letting kids be kids—it was about valuing my young life enough to not let me self-destruct. He held my life and my potential in such high regard that he was not willing to stand by and let me make decisions that could adversely impact my future. I look back and wish that more neighbors and parents today were encouraged to keep an eye on everyone else's kids in addition to their own.

Now, before all the sociologists and Al Sharpton come down on me, I certainly understand that lower-income communities may have a higher rate of crime and dysfunctional behavior for a myriad of reasons. Only 10 percent of low-income young people will go to college. There is more crime, more drug use, more teen pregnancy, more dropping out in certain parts of the country than in others. We can all agree on that.

And while economic status doesn't excuse bad behavior, of course it makes sense that certain problems thrive in certain environments. In a 2006 article, the *New York Times* reported that "terrible schools, absent parents, racism, the decline in blue-collar jobs, and a subculture that glorifies swagger over work have all been cited as causes of the deepening ruin of black youth."

Although these conditions often exist in greater numbers in inner-city neighborhoods, the phenomenon can be applied to black youth of varying geography and socioeconomic status.

This isn't solely some inevitable consequence of poverty; it's bigger than that. It is the product of a culture that is quickly losing its way. Only we can remedy absent parents, stress the importance of education to our children, lead by example by working hard, and make it a priority that our youth doesn't choose a cool pose over an education and a productive life.

It seems a two-pronged approach is necessary. First, demand excellence and accountability from all, parents and students alike. And second, for those who are having trouble, we all have a duty to step in and assist. We can no longer look at community problems from the burbs and just shake our heads in disgust and turn our backs. Everyone has a responsibility not to act a damn fool, because, contrary to popular belief, you do know better. Deal? Maybe it's just me, but there is no reason for anyone to not know any better. I firmly believe that if you don't know any better these days, then you have made a conscious decision not to.

Fortunately, lack of belief in oneself is not an irreparable problem. Self-esteem and self-empowerment can be taught. Although many youth are constantly being told what they can't do instead of what they can, we have individuals, organizations, and schools working to repair their broken confidence. There are large networks of organizations that step into the lives of these children every day and use academics, structure, and mentoring to build self-esteem and help them develop the skills they will need to succeed. The Boys and Girls Clubs of America, Kinetic Potential, Sports4Kids, Big Brothers Big Sisters, and Concerned Black Men are just a few of the programs that are on the front lines doing an amazing job at shaping the minds of the next generation.

We also live in an age where information rules. Information about anything and everything is more widely available than at any point in history. We live in an increasingly global world where information is exchanged as easily as an STD. Whether it's through the Internet, television, or other digital media, if you don't know better, you should. If you can have Facebook friends in 15 countries and follow all your favorite celebrities on Twitter, then you can find out anything you need to know. Between television and the Web, the "don't know any better" argument is ludicrous (the adjective, not the rapper).

Now what I do believe is that certain individuals suffer from a lack of belief that they *can* do better or a belief that no matter what they do, it doesn't matter. But "don't know better"? Not so much.

JAM THE NEGRO

How are you gonna expect somebody who grew up in the projects with no role models to know how to behave? Of course there are people who don't know any better. If your mama is ignorant and you don't know your daddy, then just where are you supposed to learn what is proper behavior? So there ARE people who don't know better. Sometimes where you come from dictates what you know. It's blaming the victim again. How can you blame a teenager if he or she has never had a positive influence to teach right from wrong? The teachers don't care, the parents don't care—how in the hell do you expect folks in these communities to know better? It's real easy to look down from your ivory tower and dictate what people should and should not know. You clearly have never had to fend for yourself in a world that didn't give a shit about you. Why don't you think about that? YOU should know better than to spout off about things you clearly know nothing about. Black folks in the hood don't know better because there's no one to teach them better. And you say they can learn from TV or the Internet? All everybody knows is music videos and video games, and you can't learn anything from that. Why don't you go and teach somebody something instead of talking all this smack about what people do and do not know?

JAM THE AMERICAN

Is life really that complicated? Respect. School. Work. Act like you have sense. Pretty easy stuff. I don't care if you have a bad mom or dad, at some point you know right from wrong. We play the cards we are dealt, and that means if you got a bad hand, you have to work even harder to excel. I think those who loudly kvetch about their hardships and adverse circumstances have missed a very vital development in American culture: no one cares anymore. Society and prosperity are about results. What value you bring. The reality is no one cares why you are late, why you make bad grades, why your dad left, why your mom couldn't afford new clothes for you, or why your heat wasn't on every winter and you had to use the stove for warmth. Save those stories for family, friends, and drunk chats with strangers, because the real world is about showing up and producing. When I want to make a bank deposit at 9 A.M., I could care less that your bus was late so you couldn't get to work on time. When I need to pick up my cleaning and you're late opening the store, I don't want to hear about how you overslept because you and your man were up fighting all night and your alarm didn't go off. I just want my sweater set. If I have a financial planner, I don't need to know why she's on cocaine; I don't care if her mama and daddy were dopeheads; I just need another planner. The world moves too fast and is too complicated for you to have some license to screw up and expect a bunch of back-patting from the rest of the world. Yeah, my money is fucked too, but Wachovia doesn't want to hear that. You have to realize that you are ultimately responsible for the outcome of your life. If you don't know something, find out. If you are lacking a skill, learn it. A world of information is available to you if only you have the desire to improve your condition. It's about recognizing possibilities and working hard to take full advantage of them. If one person can get out of the projects and excel, then everyone can. The victim card needs to be cut up like my over-the-limit Visa. The world is not going to coddle you; we just don't have time. If you don't know better, you should.

The "they don't know any better" excuse has far-reaching implications, particularly in the media. There is an interesting phenomenon in the media that I call the Coonery Paradox.

The Coonery Paradox—The phenomenon whereby blatant negative behavior resembling that of a coon is accepted, while critiques of that same behavior are vilified.

The black community turns a blind eye to the most coonish, negative portrayals of black folks in the media, but when those same people or stereotypes are challenged and called out for the coonery they are, the community gets into an absolute uproar, and the challenger becomes the villain.

I look at shows like *Chocolate News, The Boondocks,* and *Chappelle's Show,* all of which got heat from the black community about their portrayals of black folks and black culture. These shows cleverly satirized some of the less flattering aspects of the culture. They parodied people and situations we all know and exposed them in all their ridiculousness in a humorous way. But the message was clear. Come on, y'all! They held the mirror up and added some humor, often in an effort to challenge and ridicule the very stereotypes we supposedly hate so much. However, these shows rubbed many black folks the wrong way.

My show, *We Got to Do Better,* aimed to do the same by calling out coonish behavior for what is was: a hot-ass, embarrassing-to-us-all ghetto mess. It offered no-apologies commentary on the images of ourselves we were promulgating all over the world. It even had the nerve to have statistics and positive profiles as part of the show. And as you may or may not know, the show sparked a NATIONAL FUCKING PROTEST. The NAACP was having "watch parties," there were online petitions, panel discussions, T-shirts, and threats of sponsor boycotts. Are you serious?

Is it because there is a contingent that believes that black folks just won't get it? Do we have to be protected from anything that challenges our behavior because we just won't understand? Do we not comprehend irony or satire?

However, it is even more instructive to see the shows that go *without* protest. Where were these self-proclaimed protectors of the black image

> ❑ **Don't be afraid to challenge others to do better for fear you will sound racist or elitist. If someone is doing wrong, they are doing wrong and should be called on it, regardless of color or tax bracket.**
>
> ❑ **Don't be afraid to face and confront hard truths with respect to those you love. Though it may be tough and uncomfortable, it could help someone escape a pattern of dysfunctional and destructive behavior. Look at me—you see I don't give a shit.**

when *Flavor of Love* was on? When *Ray-J* was on? I can't think of any shows that denigrated black women like these did. There are reality shows that feature the antics of alcoholics, crackheads, and baby mamas that are put out solely for our amusement. And we don't seem to mind those one bit. No protests, no boycotts—just high ratings.

What about all the sons and daughters that will watch these shows and think they are accurate representations of black America? Shouldn't they know better? Shouldn't we show them better?

Bomani Armah is a talented artist whose animated music short "Read a Book" was a brilliant parody of the stereotypical rap video. Parents and viewers and protesters went NUTS. So wait—you are mad at the parody, but you let the real thing air all day, every day, without a peep? *I don't want that nasty parody on my television for my kids to see; show the Rick Ross video instead.*

We rarely publicly castigate those in the media who are making us all look bad, but God help you if you ever point out the fact that they're making us look bad. Then you are automatically a self-hating sellout. The Coonery Paradox.

I am by no means saying that satire and other critiques of culture shouldn't be subject to the same artistic and intellectual criticism as everything else. Let's face it—*We Got to Do Better* was no *Frank's Place*, and it wasn't exactly the show I would have liked it to be thanks to a bunch of corporate suits. But the point is, there should be a vigorous debate about all art all the time. So why are some things immediately condemned while other things consistently get a pass? I just cannot wrap my mind around the lack of public galvanization and critique of the things that are REALLY destroying the minds of our youth. The same people who hate hotghettomess.com will let their kids watch rap videos all day long.

The Coonery Paradox has at its core the "they don't know any better" rationale. We don't trust ourselves enough to allow for art that doesn't make us feel warm and fuzzy. We condemn images or stories that make us uncomfortable. We assume that our communities and our young people won't understand satire or parody or even truth. This leads to an underestimation of our intelligence as an audience. And then we wonder why we keep getting served the same schlock by Hollywood. A top executive at BET (who produced *We Got to Do Better*) told me with regard to my show's viewing audience, "They're just not ready." You know why? Because mainstream media think we don't know any better.

Let's abandon this line of thinking in the media and everywhere else. What we are doing when we dismiss people as not knowing better is treating them like children. We are essentially disrespecting a large portion of our community, deeming adults incorrigible kids. This has resulted in a huge chasm between the haves and have-nots. Instead of reaching back to assist those who have more challenges than we may have, we simply write them off as a bunch of folks who just don't know better. We write them off and walk away, leaving the problems to fester and the resentment to take hold.

On the Internet this disdain has created a virtual laughingstock of members of our community, a de facto caste system. Pathological behavior is not funny. It is not something to be forwarded around to friends for laughs to break up the monotony of the workday. On the contrary, it is a huge red flag that there are endemic problems that need serious attention as opposed to comedic Photoshop shtick. Yet still we laugh. However, let a white coworker pass around these same pictures, many of which have the subject lines "ghetto prom" or "wedding in the projects" or "get your cuzins," and we'd have our pickets signs up and race cards on the table in a New York minute.

I think the point becomes more clear if you look at it from a historical perspective. If you examine some of our most pressing issues, like the disintegration of the black family, incarceration and murder rates among black males, and high-school dropout rates, you will find that these issues actually worsened as we got richer. So did prior generations know better, and somehow now we don't? In 1940, 75 percent of black children lived with both parents. By 1990, only 33 percent lived with a mom and dad. Sociological studies show that with both parents in the home, children do better in school. The children of married people have fewer run-ins with police, have better self-esteem, and are more likely to be married themselves before having children. Somehow, 70 years ago, they got it right.

Prior generations were poorer and had less access to opportunities; however, standards for behavior, appropriate conduct, and the emphasis on education were mainstays of community and family life. They seemed to be fully aware of and to respect the fact that individualism could not be put before the collective good of the community. They understood how vital it was, in the face of racism, to be beyond reproach. They understood that any opportunities they had were hard-won and not to be taken for granted. Family and hard work were the backbone of the community and were key factors in their very survival, until family and hard work were replaced by hedonism, consumerism, nihilism, and apathy.

The state of our inner cities worsened during the exact period when blacks made some of the biggest strides. And when I say the state of our inner cities, I don't mean facts and figures—I mean the good old-fashioned state of being decent. We lost our concern for each other, our commitment to each other, our dependence on each other. It has become every man for himself, and that includes the kids. Even parenting too often takes a backseat to our personal needs. Is this because we don't know better? Or have we just opted not to do better, because it's not convenient at the time?

We often hear that inner cities and their concentrated areas of poverty and crime are the most at risk for producing generations of people who don't know better. But I would posit that city dwellers should be the last ones to use the "they don't know better" argument. With regard to residents in urban environments, to whom I hear this argument applied most often, there is usually a very present black professional class; colleges and universities abound; there are social programs aimed at self-improvement up the wazoo; and there are plenty of examples of young people overcoming odds and excelling. How can you possibly exist in this world and claim not to know any better? Maybe if you were in a rural area where everyone lived and died the same way, or in the African bush, your ignorance of the modern world could be excused.

But in a major city? Even on the bus, you see people going to work in the morning. You see men and women in suits and professional attire. But somehow I'm supposed to believe that because you grow up poor, you have absolutely no concept of working for a living and knowing right from wrong? You pass by the university and see students with books and backpacks. All the government agencies are staffed by people who look like you, and so do the bus driver, the garbage guy, and the dry cleaner. In such a diverse urban environment, the "not knowing better" argument flies in the face of logic. If there is anywhere that you see better and should know better, it's in a big city.

And frankly, wherever you are, the concepts of education, work, pride, respect, and family are pretty standard—at some point, you know right from wrong. I don't care what your socioeconomic status is, you generally know how life works. It's really not that complicated. So, instead of making this "people don't know any better" excuse, we should be talking about what it would take to reinstill a broad commitment to improving our economic and social condition in this world. The only way to make progress is to first acknowledge the problem. That's the first thing you learn in an AA meeting. (Was that too much information?)

Now, many people may not believe they CAN do better, or they may not be certain of exactly HOW to do better, or they know better and simply choose not to DO better (affectionately known as the "fuck effort" contingent). But to imply they don't know there even IS a better is a destructive theory.

Perhaps those who dismiss dysfunctional behavior as a result of blind ignorance just aren't looking at this from the proper perspective. Try this: We had an entire generation of African Americans who weren't even allowed to read, yet those were the ones who pushed most strongly for the education of their children. We had a generation of slaves who weren't allowed to marry, yet marriages and families were the foundation of the generation to follow. All it takes is the desire to improve your condition. At some point, many of us have abandoned the pursuit of improving our condition in favor of what's easy or what's fun or what's convenient or what feels good at the time. Do we know better? Of course we do. We just don't always do better. Let's call a spade a spade. No pun intended.

Generations before got it right; they understood that opportunity was valuable and took advantage of it no matter what meager circumstances they came from. Are we now saying that back then they knew better and suddenly now we don't? Generations who never had the opportunities we have now knew better and suddenly we don't? Like a bootleg DVD in a plain white envelope, I just don't buy it.

We must stop looking the other way when it comes to confronting destructive behavior simply because the person engaging in it may not be as well off as we are. When you challenge someone to do better, it is done out of love. To excuse negative acts in our community simply contributes to the absent moral compass that we are already dealing with. As we see these behaviors grow and expand at an exponential rate, it is up to the rest of the community to step in.

Former police chief of Washington, D.C., Charles Ramsey stated once, "Responsibility for your behavior has to change. We have people who just let TV and video games raise their kids and instill values . . . and then we wonder why we have a problem." Preach!

And African Americans are not as divided on this notion of personal responsibility for your destiny as the media make it seem. The Pew Research Center conducted a survey soon after Hurricane Katrina and found that most black Americans "share in the general belief in the value of hard work and are equally admiring of those that acquire wealth through it." However, if one looks at our current system of social programs in this country, these values aren't necessarily reflected. Whether geared toward urban or rural communities, many of the programs embrace the "they don't know any better" philosophical framework, which means, no matter how well meaning, they are necessarily harmful.

For example, when I worked as a lawyer in legal services, I felt that the white limo-liberals who worked there basically saw black people as children who shouldn't be expected to do anything with any level of competency. BUT we shouldn't be judged because we didn't know any better and were just hapless victims of an oppressive society and needed help. Or something like that.

Granted, those were some of the best people I had ever met, and they all were absolutely devoted to helping the less-fortunate members of society. I just don't know if spoon-feeding someone their life qualifies as helping. What was so clear to the African American lawyers there (none of whom ever stayed very long) seemed lost on our well-meaning white peers. If you treat folks like victims and tell them they have no control over the big bad world, they eventually begin to believe it. They begin to become dependent on others even when they are perfectly capable themselves. They lose the capacity to problem solve, which is essential for survival.

I saw this voluntary dependence play out every day, but one particular conversation with a gentleman stands out in my mind. I had a male client who was getting evicted, and I was able to negotiate some favorable terms to get him out of the apartment without his owing any more money. So, thirty days later, on the day he had agreed to leave the unit, he called me and asked what he was supposed to do with his furniture. I was like, What are you asking me for? And mind you, this wasn't an elderly man suffering from dementia or something; this guy was in his twenties, buff, and actually kind of fine. If he hadn't been scamming the welfare system with some fake-ass disability, I might have taken him out. But I digress.

So I thought to myself that, in the real world, whenever you move, the first thing you figure out is how you're going to move your stuff. When I asked him why he didn't make arrangements before the day he was scheduled to leave, he told me, "Well, I don't have a way to move my stuff. Don't y'all have some funds that will help me hire a mover?" I'm like, RUFKM? When I move, I have to figure it out. When my mom moves, she has to figure it out. When my friends move, they have to figure it out. You've already had a free lawyer (namely me), now you want free U-Haul services too? Negro, figure that shit out and get off my phone.

Now, did he just not know any better?

What bothered me the most was his sense of having no capacity to solve his problems, this expectation that the world owed him a solution. This sense of entitlement that he should get what he wanted without any effort on his part was so shocking. I once had a client who wanted me to fill out a form for her, when she could read and write perfectly well. I slid that form back across the desk to her, along with a blue pen. OK, you may be poor, but that means you can't write now? Everyone else in the social agency world treats them like children, but I refused. She filled the form out and kept it moving. Why? BECAUSE I REQUIRED HER TO. Seeing this type of thing over and over made me question the "they don't know better" approach and the long-term effectiveness of the liberal social program models.

Another tale from the poverty law crypt is actually a success story and was probably the definitive moment I figured out that we had it wrong. A woman, let's call her Pat, was evicted from her public housing unit (that she had been in forever and her mom had been in forever) because of a drug arrest. Public housing does not play when it comes to drug offenses on the property. She would call and ask for me to help her, help her, help her. There was nothing we could do to help her stay in that unit, and the bottom line was that she had to move. She eventually had to face this reality, and soon the calls stopped. Until about 45 days later.

When I answered the phone and realized it was Pat, I did a major eye roll. Granted, at the time, I had just gotten the wrong drink from Starbucks and was very annoyed. (You know how you don't taste it until you're half a block down the street, and then it's terrible, but you're almost to work and don't have time to go back? Exactly.)

The first thing Pat said was "I'm not calling to ask you to save my apartment. I just wanted to let you know about some of the other things that have been going on." Uh-oh. Because I'm generally disillusioned and bitter, I braced for some long convoluted tale that undoubtedly had a request for money at the end. But she surprised me. And not an "oh no, I'm pregnant" surprise but a "hey, I found $20 in my pants pocket!" surprise.

She told me that since we last talked, she had enrolled in a couple of social programs. She had begun getting some job training and was learning how to prepare to buy a home. She sounded happy, and I was happy for her. And even if she never gets a job or a home, the real prize was that she finally realized that it was in her power to get out there in this world and survive. That there was a whole world of opportunities that she had never bothered to explore because it was easier to wait on a check.

I know—it's pretty sad that a woman's eviction was the high point of my legal services career. But to see her realize that she could make it on her own was worth all the other begging assholes I had to deal with daily. Of course she had known better; she just never had any motivation to do better. And society made it easy.

As surprising as it may be, I'm not alone in my assessment of many government social programs. Research by the Pew Research Center has also shown that two-thirds of blacks share the concern that "too many low-income people are dependent on government aid." As for government programs as a whole, the polls found that blacks generally were more dubious about their efficacy than white people. Most of us know full well that many government programs aren't worth a shit.

And I know it's easier said than done. Believe me, I once received unemployment compensation, and Lord knows I didn't even think about getting a job until I had about one month left. But I knew the checks would soon end, and if I was going to eat and live, then I had to go back to work. Can you imagine living a life where the checks never end? Sucks the work ethic right out of you. The checks are killing us.

It's like tough love. It's the reason you don't give your children everything they want, even if you can. They become spoiled and unmotivated and then bring their lofty expectations and feelings of entitlement to the world, where they are sure to be disappointed. We have to stop being the spoiled brats of America. Contrary to popular belief, we know better than that.

Whew! OK, I'm done. There, I said it. So I hope that guy who called and told me that most black folks just don't know any better is reading this. People will only rise to the level of your expectations, and as long as we dismiss dysfunctional or destructive behavior as "not knowing better," we severely undercut the ability of our community to be self-sufficient, to look within to solve problems, improve conditions, and grow and prosper.

I wonder: if my bank calls and says that my car payment is late, maybe I could say that I just didn't know any better? Worth a try.

> ❑ **Never underestimate or judge anyone simply because they may be from circumstances different than your own.**

4

CALL THE MAYOR, THEN PICK UP THE TRASH YOURSELF: TRASH AS CASTE?

"Let the Negroe depend on no Party, but on himself for salvation."

—*Ida B. Wells*

So now that we've got an understanding, now that you know that excuses are unacceptable and there is no such thing as not knowing any better in this day and age, it's time for some real talk. I'm going to talk some trash, literally.

Garbage. *La basura. Déchets.*

If I see one more chicken bone, red Solo cup, box of Black and Milds, steak 'n' cheese wrapper, or blunt innard on the ground in front of my house, I'm gonna scream. If that American Indian with that one tear coming down his face who used to be in those commercials about littering stood on the corner in my neighborhood, he would need a Xanax.

I want to take some time to directly address what I call the Neighborhood Trash Illuminati (NTI). You may not have heard of them, but you've seen their work. It's like ants building an ant hill: you rarely see them in action and the only way you know they have been there is the debris they leave in their wake. They have cabals in many communities and can pervade the tightest-knit neighborhoods. The world is their trash receptacle. Who needs to be constrained to boring metal cylindrical columns when a wide sidewalk works just as well? It's so freeing to just toss your McDonald's bag into the wind and wish it well on its journey into the night air.

So when I look around at my urban neighborhood, a mirror image of every other urban neighborhood, I wonder why some of us feel so unbelievably comfortable living in filth. It's one thing if your home is fucked up inside. But why do you have to subject the rest of us to your trashy ways?

It comes back to standards and expectations. Of course, this isn't really about trash; it is about a state of mind. It's about owning our destiny, and part of that is owning our surroundings. I'm not talking about literally owning. (I mean, after those ARMs adjusted, who were we fooling?) I'm talking about having pride in our communities and accountability for how we live, no matter where that may be or what your ownership status.

Much like your personal appearance, the way you treat your surroundings is a reflection of you. The way you maintain your home says a lot about how you view your own value. So, if the way we live is a representation of ourselves, why do we often treat our communities with such disregard?

The two most common responses I get to this query are

1. *if an area is poor, it's gonna be filthy;*
2. *the city discriminates—it doesn't clean predominantly minority areas the way it cleans majority white areas.*

Let me take on both of these cop-outs.

When in the hell did it become fact that poverty = filth? Or does that theory just make us all feel better about doing nothing to challenge this behavior because it is somehow preordained, genetic, inevitable? *Oh well, nothing we can do about that. Poor folks are just going to throw shit on the ground.*

Not only is this a cop-out, it is absolutely insulting to anyone of modest means who treats his or her environment with respect and pride. Being poor is not some "fuck up for free" card.

The "poverty = filth" stance is just a variation on the "they don't know any better" argument. Somehow we feel that if someone doesn't have much money, he or she automatically becomes a filthy person with no regard for his or her surroundings. That's outrageous and insulting. There are plenty of people without much money whose floors you could eat off, and conversely there are some wealthy folks who are nasty as hell.

We should all be responsible for the things we *do* control in our lives. Perhaps we can't change our schools or our health care options or the social services in our community, but we *can* affect our own homes and neighborhoods. It doesn't take money to care what your home looks like. It doesn't cost a thing to pick up the trash in front of your building or get rid of the debris in your front yard. And it's absolutely free of charge for you to clean the crap off the floor in the living room.

This isn't about trivial vanity. It's about creating an atmosphere of excellence. It's about maintaining a quality of life and a standard of living that demonstrate the high regard you have for yourself. And it's not only about you; children need to know that we care enough about them to create a safe, inviting, warm environment for them.

You teach children an important lesson when you take the time and energy to take care of your home and neighborhood. You teach them to value their surroundings. When you enforce a standard of cleanliness and order in the home, you really say to them, "I care too much about you to allow you to live in filth." Children learn what they live, and when they see you pick up a wayward grape soda can in front of the house and dispose of it properly, it speaks volumes about how you should treat your home.

I remember my mom would pick up any stray piece of trash from the yard, and at the time I was grossed out at the thought of her picking up someone else's trash. However, she explained that it wasn't about the trash; it was about our home and our community. She'd ask, "Would you rather just leave all the trash in the yard so we could come home to a front yard full of garbage every day?" Even now, that question rings in my head as I debate in my mind whether to pick up that brown bag in front of my house, speculating on all the horrid things that might be in it. Would I rather just leave it there and come home to it everyday? Nope, Mom, I would not.

It is our responsibility to take every opportunity to make our communities better places to live. We all have a vested interest in creating beauty. We value what is beautiful. It's like L'Oréal: we're worth it. And our children are worth it. Let's not raise a generation to have no regard for its own neighborhoods. Let's teach young people by example, which means not throwing that McDonald's bag (cup and all) out of the car window. Even if it's not your neighborhood, it's someone else's.

- ❑ Teach your children to have pride in their surroundings. Involve them in picking up trash, in painting, and in other neighborhood beautification activities. You get their fat asses off the couch and the block gets improved. It's win-win.

- ❑ Put just as much energy into your home and surrounding areas as you do your clothes, car, and hurr.

- ❑ Your home and neighborhoods are a reflection of you. Show your children that you care how they live.

No matter what some liberal excusists may say, this has nothing to do with economics. We all should be held to the same high standards regardless of our financial strata. It doesn't cost a damn thing not to throw trash on the ground, so why should people think this is some inherent trait of the poor or working class? This type of condescending thinking allows us to sit back and wave off bad behavior as some sort of genetic predisposition like breast cancer or alcoholism. The trash caste is of no particular age, economic status, or color. The only commonality is a complete disregard of their surroundings, whether it's their home, street, or someone else's property.

And though this may seem like nothing more than a trivial nuisance, it's surprising how complex the trash issue becomes with respect to race and class.

I live in a neighborhood that is in the midst of full-on gentrification. So for the first time in my lifetime, I have a significant number of white neighbors. The community has become not only ethnically diverse but also economically diverse. You have million-dollar homes next to boardinghouses next to coffeehouses next to condos next to crack houses next to art galleries next to low-income rentals. In other words, it's generally a clusterfuck.

There is an apartment building in my neighborhood that I pass on my dog-walking route, and without fail, there are always chicken bones in front of it. My unofficial say-in-my-head name for it is the CBA— Chicken Bone Apartments. And it's more than just an aesthetic annoyance: my dog gets into the bones, and then I have to wrestle a greasy, sucked-on drumstick out of my dog's mouth in 90-degree heat. He has even developed a Pavlovian response when he approaches this particular block—his excitement is obvious as he walks, anticipating a quick bone nibble before I can intervene.

So anyway, I run into one of my white neighbors, "Jim." He is also a dog owner, and we often talk in passing about our canine companions. (Because, like most neighbor-to-neighbor relationships in the 21st century, that's all we really know about each other.) So one day I run into him shortly after passing the CBA and wrestling several chicken-wing bones from my dog. Sure, I was a little miffed. So I speak to him and start expressing my frustration at our neighbors leaving so much litter and food waste outside of their apartment building.

So here I am, in the midst of an inner-city neighborhood talking to this white yuppie about my neighbors in this apartment building (of whom 99.998 percent are black), about the problem of chicken bones and trash outside of the building. It was so fraught with unspoken racial undertones. On one hand I almost felt guilty for talking to him about this, which no doubt reinforces stereotypes he might have and has certainly heard about black folks. But on the other hand, why can't I talk to a neighbor about a problem that affects everyone in the community?

It's that damn DuBois duality again. How can I implore my neighbors to keep the place clean and chicken bone free without feeling like I'm betraying some black chicken brotherhood? And on the flip side, if a white person mentions that there are too many chicken bones on the sidewalk, he's viewed as making a stereotypical, racist comment. So in the end we all just tolerate living in a sea of chicken bones because mentioning them is a lose-lose situation.

I am so tired of bad behavior getting a pass because the perpetrators are black and/or poor. Everyone is so uncomfortable with the conversational undertones that we all play it safe. No one says anything. So the community-wide conversations we should be having are relegated to hushed conversations at dinner tables, beauty salons, barbershops, and happy hours. And then when you publicly call out the behavior, in this case the constant littering of chicken bones, soda bottles, and carryout leftovers, you immediately get called an elitist who is blaming the victim. The victim? The only victim I see here is me for having to navigate through your trash to get down the sidewalk.

The other explanation (read: "excuse") as to why there is more litter and debris in our urban neighborhoods is that the city doesn't clean the streets in minority communities like they do in other areas. I believe that is true. No doubt there is racism. Black life is devalued and often marginalized. There is also classism. Inequality exists in the level of services the city provides to high-income areas versus low-income areas regardless of race. Yes, yes, a thousand times yes.

However, these ongoing inequalities do not negate the need to act on your own behalf to improve yourself or your neighborhood. It is not an either/or situation. Lobbying for equality of opportunity and services and emphasizing personal responsibility are not mutually exclusive. Of course, we should lobby our cities for high-quality services, but while we are waiting for our letters to the mayor to be answered, we should get out there and pick up the damn trash ourselves. To allow conditions in our communities to deteriorate while waiting for the government cavalry to rush in for a rescue is outrageous. We should never stop holding the government accountable, but in the meantime we can focus on what part we can play in solving the problem.

Of course we should all speak loudly, carry big sticks, and demand the services that our tax dollars entitle us to. But as we fight The Man, we can also put an equal amount of energy into organizing, mobilizing, getting our trash bags, and solving the problem ourselves. Even in high-income communities, residents are not afraid to organize a trash pickup where everyone wears shorts and

> ❏ Hold your government accountable for its responsibilities to its citizenry, but don't be slaves to it. Enacting changes on your own and asking your government to act are not mutually exclusive.
>
> ❏ Don't go through life waiting to be rescued. So many people are so focused on being rescued, they miss the fact that they can save themselves.

old T-shirts, takes up Glad bags and sticks with points on the end, and spends Saturday taking care of the neighborhood. Best believe, they are phoning and e-mailing the city as well, but they refuse to drown in garbage while waiting for a response.

Let's stop acting like helpless children. We are the descendants of the strongest of the strong. We are the progeny of men and women who struggled and fought and sacrificed and survived the greatest crime against humanity ever. And we can't pick up a goddamned Burger King bag?

> ❏ Pride in your home, yourself, and your street has nothing to do with money. Poverty = filth is a myth. The *Good Times* apartment was neat as a pin.

There seems to be a strange correlation between debris-filled streets and the way we live. As we continue to celebrate the gritty and grimy, as we obsess over realness, bling, thuglife, and whoredom, our streets are following suit. The effects of our "anything goes" philosophy are being felt not only in the way we live our personal lives but how we treat the world around us. Our communities should be a place our children can be proud of. We should instill the importance of pride in one's surroundings in our kids. But how can our kids learn the importance of pride in their homes when they see Mama throwing her shrimp lo mein out of the window?

JAM THE NEGRO

This is outrageous. How are you gonna sit there and blame a bunch of poor people for the condition of their neighborhood? These are areas that the city has neglected for years, and now you want the residents, who are trying their best to survive, to be responsible for street cleaning? I guess they should all buy trash trucks, too, right? We need to hold the government accountable and not give it a pass for its systematic neglect of the black community. The answer is lobbying for our rights, not chastising the community because it is not doing something the government is obliged to do. We have enough responsibilities just trying to make it day to day without donning a hazmat suit and power washing the damn curbs. We pay taxes just like everyone else, so why shouldn't we get the services we pay for? The government just doesn't care about our neighborhoods, and it's about time everyone rallied, forcing government action instead of blaming the victims of its neglect. Maybe all those people picking up trash on the weekend in their fancy neighborhoods don't have kids to raise. They can get their nannies to do it while they are out singing "Kumbaya" and recycling, but I have a job and kids and too many responsibilities to add cleaning up the city to my to-do list.

JAM THE AMERICAN

Oh, give me a break. The Man isn't the one who is coming to your front stoop and tossing around chicken bones. As mentioned earlier, you can petition the government for improved services—and, at the same time, pick up the trash. There are plenty of neighborhoods, rich and poor, that organize Saturday trash pickups in order to clean up the block. What makes you so special? If someone doesn't do it for you, then guess what, you have another option: do it for yourself! Sure, it would be great if the government treated all its citizens equally, but trust, you living in squalor is not punishing the government. The only people who suffer are the residents (and particularly the children) of these communities, who are never taught the value of investing one's time and energy into beautifying their surroundings. So they continue the cycle. If the government drops the ball and you are able to pick it up, why wouldn't you? Why is doing nothing considered a viable option? 'Cause you're mad? Join the club. My stepdad used to tell me when I was growing up, "If you're mad, scratch your ass and be glad." We have gotten into this pathological cycle of dependency where we've been asking for things for so long, we don't even realize that we can solve our own problems. Government help is like Godot. And we cannot keep waiting.

So, to the Neighborhood Trash Illuminati I say, whether your preference is Grey Poupon or Mambo Sauce, when you finish licking your lips, rubbing your belly, sucking your fingers, and wiping your mouth, please think of your neighbors and your neighbors' dogs and your neighbors' property values and toss your refuse in an appropriate location. It benefits everyone to live in clean, safe neighborhoods. While some may find a certain charm in stepping over carryout leftovers, empty 40-ounce bottles, chicken bones, cigarette butts, blunt guts, and weed Baggies, most of us do not.

By implementing a few simple strategies, we can elevate our neighborhoods to places where adults and children alike can learn, play, thrive, and grow.

Eliminate the "wun't me" attitude. OK, I know you may not have dropped it, but it's sitting right in front of your home. Would it kill you to pick it up? I have to pick up trash and other debris that flies into my yard or crosses my path daily. It's not about you; it's about maintaining clean streets where we live. You must care about your world enough to know that picking up the peach Nehi bottle is the right thing to do. Even if it wun't you that dropped it.

Organize! Every month, get a bunch of your neighbors and the neighborhood kids up and out to do a community cleanup. Get some trash bags and old clothes and tackle those streets. It's a great way to meet your neighbors, get some exercise, and clean shit up. Kids not only have an active and productive way to spend an afternoon, they also see an entire neighborhood acting together. They're learning that clean streets and respect for where you live are important. You can also use organized events to paint over graffiti, maintain abandoned lawns, or tend to any other community eyesores.

And just maybe your neighbors are a bunch of ne'er-do-wells who could care less about your stupid cleanup event. They take your flyer that you lovingly created on Microsoft Publisher and throw it in the recycle box with the rest of the junk mail. Well, to hell with them. Get your family or a bunch of your friends, fix some cocktails, and do it your damn self. All it takes is some cheap trash bags, some gloves, and the desire to make your community the best it can be.

Get involved! Become a part of your neighborhood organizations. Make your voice heard when it comes to decision making regarding your community. Have a say in what businesses move into your area, make authorities aware of crimes specific to your neighborhood, and get to know your neighbors.

I know, I know. Who wants to sit in some hot-ass church basement with a bunch of old biddies who have nothing to do but complain about what color Ms. Jones painted her garage or why Harry has so many female overnight guests? Ah well, it's the price we must pay for making a difference. We *must* get involved. These organizations often are long overdue for an injection of energy, new ideas, and fresh perspectives.

Our neighborhoods are reflections of us. Pride should be exhibited not only in how you look and behave but also in how you live. Excellence should be the standard. It's not going to happen overnight, and it will not happen without effort. But there is no doubt that we can improve our communities. And not only can we bring light and pride back to our neighborhoods, but we can also teach our kids to do the same. We will raise a generation that values its homes and the homes of its neighbors. Litterers will become the outcasts, and a clean living space will be the ultimate fashion statement.

And maybe, just maybe, when the mayor finally answers our letters, we can say, "Never mind, we've taken care of it ourselves."

5

IF YOU'RE GONNA HANG
ON THE CORNER ALL DAY,
TAKE A BOOK
(MITIGATE YOUR DAMAGES)

"Mistakes are a fact of life . . . it is the response to the error that counts." —*Nikki Giovanni*

OK, so we all make mistakes. We've all had our share of failures in life. Lord knows I've had mine: the porno letter-writing business, my tax class in law school, the cashless ATM scheme, dating that married guy, or when I got Beyoncé fever and dyed my hair blonde in '04. *But* mistakes, even a series of them (and OK—maybe the same one over and over again), do not necessarily mean the end of the world and, most important, do not give you license to wallow in perpetual dysfunction.

We all make decisions that we wish we could take back. Sometimes these choices have a profoundly negative impact and make our lives infinitely more difficult. Maybe you dropped out of school, maybe you had a child with some cad before you were ready, maybe you kept it too real and ended up in the clink. But you can't allow regret and bitterness to extinguish your hopes and dreams of a better life for yourself and your children. So you screwed up; now what?

Well, you have two options: (1) you can feel sorry for yourself and whine and complain, or (2) you can mitigate the messes you've made by using the opportunities available to you. Whether you were born with the deck stacked against you or you have managed to fuck up your life all by yourself, bitching and moaning about what you don't have should not be a life strategy.

Let's face it: no one really gives a shit about you. No one wants to hear you drone on about how hard life is, why you can't make it, or what you cannot do.

The days of benevolence, charity, and coddling are over. It's sink or swim, survival of the fittest, fight or flight, and all those other anthropological clichés. Brother's keepers, much like Commodore 64s and Intellivision, are things of the past. Everyone's job is shaky, money is funny, credit is bad, pressure is high—everyone has their own problems. I mean, do you really think people enjoy your two-hour "poor me" conversations late at night? No offense, I'm just telling you this because your friends, family, and coworkers are way too nice to tell you the truth.

So, where does that leave you? It leaves you where you have always been. Absolutely capable of figuring things out and moving forward.

Winston Churchill once said, "If you're going through hell, keep going." We simply cannot allow our mistakes to consume us to the point where we define ourselves by our failures. This persistent unconscious identification with playing the victim prevents us from absorbing the wealth of opportunity that surrounds us. We can't allow our present circumstances to dictate our potential in this world. There are many resources available to help rebuild our lives, but we are so busy concentrating on what we cannot do, what we don't have, how bad things are for us, and what someone else has that we can't see the world of opportunity awaiting anyone who wishes to go out and get it. Cornel West once stated, "The major enemy of black survival in America has been and is neither oppression nor exploitation but rather the nihilistic threat—that is, loss of hope and absence of meaning."

We must recalibrate the meaning of success in our lives. For the last two decades we've measured success in bling and things. Our relentless pursuit of stuff has often been stronger than our pursuit of education, healthy families, and strong communities. Our image of success has changed. Somewhere between *The Cosby Show* and *Flavor of Love*, we lost our way.

Striving for goals that are fleeting, things that depreciate, activities that sap our integrity and diminish us lead us on a search for something we will never find: a true sense of self. We are lost, so we begin to regress, feeling helpless and unsure of who we are and what we're about. We have little faith in ourselves, so we begin to wait for the cavalry or for the magical Negro (depending on what part of the country we're in) to figure it all out for us. In the meantime we'll just complain to anyone who will listen until someone gives us what we want. No more.

There are no excuses. It is time for us to realize we have the potential to turn our condition around one person at a time, even if we've done a piss-poor job at managing our lives thus far.

Although it's hard to hear sometimes, everything isn't someone else's fault. The truth is, your life probably isn't difficult because you're a woman, because you're a man, because you live in your neighborhood, because you're black, because you're white, because you're Latino, because you're light skinned or dark skinned, because of who your mama was or where you went to school. Take a real slow look at your life, particularly at things you consider your failures,

- ❑ Life isn't fair. Get over it.
- ❑ It's never too late to do anything.

and ask yourself how you got there. Nine times out of ten you'll find that you just fucked up. Bad decision here, bad relationship there, bad money move here—it happens. Sometimes the person to blame is right in the mirror. The good thing about that is that if you are the cause of your condition, then you have the power to reverse your fortune. Hopelessness, blame, and bitterness are all just impediments to a better life for you and your family.

An obsession with a hard life is what traps so many of us in the death grip of hopelessness. We don't try to be better, simply because things have been so bad. However, in comparison with our brothers and sisters around the world, many of us have no idea what a hard life is. I talk to many immigrants from the Caribbean and from African countries who are greatly impressed by African Americans' ability throughout history to overcome enormous odds to progress to where we are today. They marvel at the strides we have made as a race in a relatively short period of time against seemingly insurmountable odds. *However*, they are nonplussed at African Americans' constant complaining and sense of entitlement.

I spoke to a brother from South Africa who couldn't understand why so many blacks here drop out of school and do not work. He had the view that work is easy—poverty is what is hard. And in this country, while we are quick to play the poverty card, he said that we can't begin to understand what real poverty is. He noted that Americans who are considered poor have microwaves and cars and satellite TVs and cell phones. He said his relatives have dirt floors and no running water. If these people, along with those in similar communities all over the world, could have hope and perseverance and the desire to work and improve their condition, then how do we dare be hopeless and bitter while we sit in our air-conditioned homes on our leather sofas, wearing $200 sneakers, and driving our Chrysler 300s while talking on our cell phones?

Unlike so many people in nations around the world, we have the ability to change our circumstances. We can stop, reflect, and decide to change the direction of our lives at any time. We are not slaves to a caste system; we are not subjects of an oppressive religious regime that dictates our behavior and potential in life based on what genitalia we were born with. Our view of our own potential and opportunity seems so myopic and so incongruent with reality.

It seems that everyone except black folks sees America as a land of opportunity. We look at it askance, like it owes us money. And, of course, considering our history of slavery and Jim Crow and violence and discrimination and shit like the Tuskegee experiment, we definitely have adequate grounds for a beef with the United States. However, we can't let this anger at our past stifle our future. And if you are going to be angry, be a *productively* angry citizen. There's nothing worse than someone sitting on their ass, just being angry.

When I look around me, so many of my neighbors' and classmates' and coworkers' problems have nothing to do with racism. I know there are those who can find racism when the grocery store is out of mayonnaise. But seriously, if you decided to drop out of school and use your student loan money to get a car, if you financed a house you couldn't afford, if you had a baby or two with some idiot, if you ran up your credit card on expensive purses or Remy hair weaves, the person at the center of those decisions generally isn't the Grand Wizard of the KKK. It's you! And that's a good thing!

As long as we feel that failure is inevitable because of race or socioeconomic status, we will never open our eyes to all the things that can be achieved with perseverance and a little hard work. Remember hard work? This sense that someone owes you something "just because" is sooo '90s.

This strange marriage of victimhood and entitlement can be seen in the differentiation between African Americans' view of the United States and many immigrant populations'. While many immigrants come to America seeing a land of opportunity where the road to success is paved by hard work, we sometimes see it as an IOU in the shape of a country. I know, it's a little annoying having to navigate all the Latino men in the Home Depot parking lot when you just went in looking for a couple of citronella candles for the deck, *but* I have to admire anyone who is out there hustling for work. I'd much rather see someone clamoring to do home improvement than the guy at the busy intersection with a Styrofoam cup or the eight young men standing on my corner all day. They could at least paint a fence while they're out there. Damn.

Life's a bitch, absolutely. Slavery and racism are bad, bad, bad. But what's next? I find it almost amusing that many young people today who never got called "nigger," never had to enter from the back of a hotel, and never had to go to segregated schools are the main ones crying racism. We grew up on *The Cosby Show,* for chrissakes. These Negroes make a racist fuss about cabs that don't pick them up. I wouldn't pick up your thug-life ass, either.

It's very important to me to retain a sense of reverence and pride for our history but not use it as an eternal excuse for failure. As I said earlier, my parents—like many others of their generation—told us that we had to be twice as good as our white counterparts in order to be considered equal. Do you realize how important that message is? It simultaneously acknowledges the difficulties of racism and challenges children to defeat it with excellence and hard work.

Look at the Jewish community. They won't let you forget about the Holocaust, but they don't show their protest of genocide with whining and moaning and using it as an excuse to be poor and broke down. They show it with strength and resilience. Like we once did, pre-NWA.

In Bill Cosby's book *Come On People,* he talks about changing your attitude from victim to victor. He's absolutely right. So your life is a mess; instead of using all your energy to figure out why it's someone else's fault, figure out how you can use the resources provided by your city, your family, and your friends to turn things around. You should want your children to witness resilience and not just apathy and nihilism. Show them that every setback is not a disaster, that they have the power to change the game with dedication and a little hustle. (By "hustle" I mean hard work, not "a hustle," à la the three-card monte.) Standing around waiting for some external force to rescue us is a recipe for disaster, setting a dangerous example to our children.

It's all about mitigating your damages. In law, mitigating your damages is something required of everyone who brings a suit. It simply means that you can't just sit around and rack up damages so you can sue for more money. You must take the initiative to limit the amount of damage that you incur. We should all do the same when approaching life.

Don't wallow; don't complain. Act! Over the years, I went to school with and worked with so many people whose stories of hardships would bring tears to your eyes. I worked with a single mother who went from food stamps and welfare to attending one of the most prestigious law schools in the country. She ultimately became an attorney for one of the biggest law firms in the world. She often sat and talked to me about her challenges and about how one day she decided she would not be another statistic.

She put her nose to the grindstone, spent all night, every night, studying for her LSATs, and, as a result, kicked ass on them. She used all the resources available to her to make her situation better and position herself for success in the future. Was the road rough? Yes. Was it rougher than all her classmates'? Hell, yes. But she did it. And she lives to preach about the value of working hard and challenging your condition. Sure, she made some mistakes that made her road bumpier than it needed to be, but she had two choices: (1) wallow in regret, or (2) suck it up, work harder, and keep reaching for the sky. She kept reaching, and she is a constant reminder to me when I face adversity in my

❑ As interested as people seem to be in what you are saying, they are secretly tired as hell of your complaining.

❑ When you start complaining and bitching and whining, stop and think of those who have it worse than you do. And if that doesn't work, think of your ancestors who would have been thrilled if their worst problems were late child support payments, bad credit, and a subprime mortgage. Puts it all in perspective, huh?

life. Whenever I get the urge to curse the gods for my misfortune, I stop and think of her, and then I feel like a fool.

There are so many of these stories. I know a single dad who managed to attend a top graduate school while caring for a young daughter. He graduated and started his own business so he would be able to spend more time with her. Even though he keeps his eye on the prize and knows one day he will get his business off the ground, he still struggles daily with his basic needs and has had to sacrifice many of the trappings his friends are able to enjoy. It was a tough road for him and it continues to be, but he understands that the most important thing he can give his daughter is his time, and he is determined to make her the priority, no matter what. He finds solace in the fact that he puts his daughter first and knows that will reap rewards greater than any paycheck.

Challenges, tough times, and mistakes don't have to be a death sentence. Sure, sometimes you look up and, for whatever reason, your life is a disaster. Let's talk about what you don't do first.

Even if it is his fault, don't blame the White Man. It gets you nowhere. And no one wants to hear it. People might look like they are paying attention to your griping, but all we're really thinking about is how it's your fault and that you're full of shit, or how much the string in our new thong is irritating our ass.

I don't mean to get all Napoleon Hill on you (don't worry, I won't tell you to visualize anything), but life isn't always easy. Only your own persistence and the belief that you can succeed can change your destiny. Success and happiness don't just happen; you can't get them from a Lucky Three scratch card. The solutions to your problems aren't in a dream book or at the corner store. The solutions are in your marvelous mind. You *could* sit and wallow about how you're too black, or too whatever, and that life isn't fair and that the world owes you something, but a fat lotta good that's done you so far, huh?

JAM THE NEGRO

Oh, well lookie here. You finally decided to encourage positive change instead of blindly criticizing everything everybody else is doing. But what you fail to point out is that black people will never be able to rise to their full potential in a racist country. The institutional racism that exists everywhere from the school system to the legal system is designed to keep black folks in a subordinate position. Yeah, you can take your little classes and read your books and pretend that you are living the AmeriKKKan dream, but in reality you're just fooling yourself. Our lives won't get better until someone is held accountable for the state of black America in every city in this nation. You think all these black men in prison just magically appeared there? It's a conspiracy to rid our communities of our strongest black warriors. It's hard to hear naive black people like you talk because you are an example of how the brainwashing of modern black folks has taken hold. You really think white America is gonna give you any real power? I don't care how many languages you learn or therapy sessions you attend or continuing education classes you go to in the evenings, the only way we can rise up as a people is to collectively challenge this repressive regime called the United States of America. You are trying to shoot a bear with a BB gun.

JAM THE AMERICAN

Please. Unless you are planning some armed revolution by American Negroes (which will never happen because we will NOT miss *House of Payne* UNDER ANY CIRCUMSTANCES), then all of your talking is moot. Sure, this is a country built on the backs of our ancestors. Yes, racism and classism pervade every aspect of society. OK, now what? Are you telling me you would rather sit around and gripe about The Man instead of taking action on your own behalf? Are you waiting for Jesus Christ to descend from the heavens and create a color-blind world for you to live in? No one says you shouldn't continue to fight for equality, but in the meantime, work to create a better world for yourself and your family. Do you think that wallowing in anger and protest is punishing anyone? The solution to racism isn't protest; it's excellence. That was something our forefathers realized. They fought for their rights while excelling in education and working hard. You can't fight the system while sitting on your ass. How dare you try to demean me for encouraging people to change their lives for the better? You probably would have told Oprah, "Girl, that white man ain't ever gonna let you host a TV show. Girl, that white man ain't ever gonna let you own your own magazine. Girl, that white man ain't ever gonna let you make a billion dollars." If it were up to you, Oprah would be in the projects waiting on checks because you'd have convinced her that her dreams were subject to the whim of the white man's racism. Our dreams are actually about us. Our quest for excellence and integrity and success is more powerful than anyone's prejudices, especially in today's world. So stop focusing on what you can't do or what happened to you. If your life is fucked up, don't blame; don't bitch—get off your ass and get to fixing it.

Bill Cosby, in an interview with Juan Williams for Williams's book *Enough*, outlined some very simple steps to take to improve your odds for success: go to school, get a job and keep it, and marry before you have a baby. Sounds simplistic, huh? It's almost frightening that such a simple solution to problems seems to have escaped a large segment of our population. Well, the poverty rate for black Americans who take these steps is 6.4 percent. The overall poverty rate for black Americans is 21.5 percent. Sounds like a good plan to me. I'm no sociologist and I don't play one on TV, but I do know that making smart choices is key. Inject some common sense into your life's plan. Doing what you want and leaving it up to Jesus is some bullshit. Jesus won't have to raise those four kids by three dads. But even if you have made some questionable choices, even if the road is more difficult for you, success is never impossible. The prolific poet Nikki Giovanni said, "Mistakes are a fact of life/It is the response to the error that counts."

We must rally around ourselves. We must tap into our internal Barack Obamas and organize huge Change rallies in our hearts and minds. There are so many outlets available to us for change and improvement. Between the nonprofit world and government programs, there is always someone out there to help you make the changes you need to make in your life. It just takes the effort to seek out the appropriate channels. Perhaps you need access to information, assistance navigating the legal process, financial planning, financial aid for going back to school, a literacy program, or help from a mental health or social work professional—believe me, it's out there. And, sure, the programs may not be as efficient or organized as they could be, and the wait may be lengthy, but these people are there to help you. Take advantage. No one is going to force you to self-correct. That comes from within. The desire to improve comes from the knowledge that you have the ability to rise above any challenge and improve the condition of your life and the lives of those close to you.

You don't always have to participate in a formal program to learn something. Self-improvement is often as simple as seeking out people in the community for advice or assistance. Look at those around you whom you would like to emulate in some way, and sit down with them. Talk to them about how they got where they are. They will be flattered, and you will gain some useful insight and information.

You don't always have to have a problem in order to take measures to improve your quality of life. Sometimes it might just be fun to take a free class on a new topic or new language or read that book you heard about or check out a documentary instead of the latest Wayans Brothers comedy (not that there's anything wrong with the Wayans). Believe me, any money spent on self-improvement goes much further than a new TV set or renting a table in the VIP room.

Seeking out assistance to improve your condition is nothing to be ashamed of. Maintaining a certain coolness, unflappability, and a brick-hard emotional veneer often keeps us from getting the help we need. We think asking for help makes us look weak. Some of us even hold up our failures as badges of honor. Failure isn't cute; it isn't funny; it isn't gangsta. It's stupid. Our ancestors died so we could be exposed to opportunities. Ignoring a pathway out of dysfunction or poverty for the sake of a sneer and a cool pose is the ultimate insult to those brave men and women.

As black folks, we often feel the need to come across strong and steadfast because we've been vulnerable for so long. But there is dignity in grabbing on to that ladder and pulling yourself out of bad situations. There is pride in overcoming obstacles and working hard for what you have. Is someone going to tap you on the shoulder and force upon you chances and opportunities and a better life? No.

Will you find a better life in a settlement, disability, or welfare check? NO.

Will you find a better life standing around talking shit on the corner? NO.

Will you find a better life doing the same old thing the same old way? NO.

Read this slowly: no one is responsible for making your life better but you. Life is not about what someone gives you; it's about what you can take for yourself.

6

IT TAKES
A VILLAGE,
MY ASS

"The children are our future. Unless we stop them now."
—Homer Simpson

"Morality and values begin at home. If Black America is to continue its greatness, it must take care of its children."
—Alvin Poussaint

Can I just talk to y'all, one villager to another?

I know the saying "it takes a village to raise a child" sounds all good and profound in that wise-old-African-man kind of way, but I'm a little confused about its practical application these days.

There seems to be some sort of misunderstanding between the village children and the village elders. Something has gone wrong. For example, I was walking my dog Albert in the neighborhood when I came upon some kids walking down the street toward me. They were singing, "Kevin and Nikki sitting in a tree, F-U-C-K-I-N-G." Now, while that is pretty appalling, as these were nine- and ten-year-olds, it wasn't as appalling to me as the fact that they were willing to say this right in front of an adult.

That's the difference I see between kids today and kids I grew up with. I'm certainly not going to sit here all holier-than-thou like I was never a badass kid. I played all the freaky games, tripped up other kids, and developed a shocking affinity for profanity around age eight. However, I would NEVER have considered cursing around adults or doing any of my mischief in their presence. What happened to adult authority? What happened to kids being afraid of adults? The fact that these kids could care less about what they were saying and who heard them was really scary.

I'm sure we all have our similar stories. We've all been walking down the street or on the bus or subway with young people who have no qualms about loudly using cusswords or n-words or openly discussing their sexual exploits, both real and imagined. I used to ride the bus to work, and the language these kids shouted in front of small children, women, and the elderly was S-H-O-C-K-I-N-G.

Since when did it become their world? A world where they can speak to you any kind of way? When did an adult become just another person in their way, just another person they decide to ignore?

I certainly don't underestimate the difficulty and challenges of raising a child in today's world. I can't imagine what 21st century parents deal with when trying to groom and shape a child in the age of YouTube, Ritalin, MySpace, oral-sex-as-recreation, globalization, and cell phones. HOWEVER, parents should have thought of all that before they decided to have children. So, either rise to the occasion and do what you have to do, OR tie your damn tubes. It's called Plan B. You can get it over-the-counter now.

I'm not sure what happened, but sometime in the last 20 years, we have totally lost control of our young people. How did the paradigm change so drastically and we all missed it? One morning, kids were kids, and the next morning they are asking you, "What the fuck are you looking at?" Somehow kids have this crazy sense that adults are merely their taller, fatter peers. And they act accordingly.

This children-rule-the-world framework is often reinforced by popular culture. Whereas once we had *The Cosby Show* and *Good Times* and even *Roseanne*, where the parents were in full control and always won, now we have The Disney Channel and Nickelodeon and a slew of sitcoms and films that portray parents as clueless dodos that exist merely for the children's amusement and ridicule. Fathers have become Homer Simpson and mothers have become Peggy Bundy. The kids are running the show, defying the rules, and calling all the shots.

It's tough. We no longer live in a society that reinforces parental control. Society acts in absolute opposition to that theory, and our children are eating it up. Add to that the fact that many children are growing up with single parents or two working parents and thus have a lot of alone time on their hands. Between the time they spend by themselves and the indulgence showered on them by parents who feel guilty because of the lack of time they are able to spend with their kids, is there any wonder they are running wild?

Granted, the family as a whole has changed. Today the norm is either two working parents or a single-parent household. This challenges us to face familial and parenting issues we never had to deal with growing up. In many ways we're flying by the seat of our pants.

My hat goes off to the parents of the world. It's the hardest job there is, and so many of them are doing an outstanding job in the face of extraordinary social and financial challenges. HOWEVER, some of them are also failing miserably. One prime example of a parenting failure is the best-friend scenario. Be it a two-working-parent family or a single-parent home, parents have suddenly decided to become BFs with their kids. The children are constantly catered to, appeased, and pacified. It's their world and you're just living in it. As long as they're not mad at you, everything is OK. You just don't want any trouble. You're tired. You feel guilty that you're not there for them because you're working all the time, so you shower them with gifts and privileges. Your presents say, "Please don't hate me." Peace at any cost. A Pyrrhic victory indeed.

Parents aren't the only culprits, though. For years, mainstream media has portrayed children as the only ones in a household with any sense. The mother is often depicted as being well intentioned but clueless, the father a doofus. From the crib, children learn that the power is theirs. The world exists to make them happy.

Sure, young people are by nature egocentric—it's a survival mechanism—but as they grow up, it seems parents continue to reinforce to them that they are indeed the center of the universe, and everyone should treat them as such. Children don't feel the need to defer to anyone or to respect anyone. There is no longer a clear distinction between the world of adults and the world of children. They see the world as one big peer group. Is it any surprise when they are screwed up by 16? And it's everyone's fault but theirs.

> ❏ **Be a parent. Fuck friendship.**

Everyone suddenly started parenting like Oprah and Dr. Phil. When Oprah came out against corporal punishment on her show, I knew we were in trouble. And when you combine that with the Dr. Phil method of parenting by negotiation, you've got a recipe for disaster. I was watching an episode of Dr. Phil recently, and he was doing a show on how to negotiate with your kids to get them to do things. I was like, "negotiate"? What happened to "because I told you so"? Sometime in the last 10 years, we decided that our children were our friends and that, for fear of hurting their precious feelings, we should defer to them on everything. Everything they do is right, and everyone else is wrong. This new parenting revolution that stresses negotiation, conversation, and friendship with your kids, as opposed to the because-I-said-so/beat-that-ass parenting style of yore is taking us all right down the shitter.

Of course, it's not all Oprah's and Dr. Phil's fault. There are a variety of factors that contribute to our out-of-control youth and our apathetic, lazy parenting. When 50 percent of African American households are headed by a single parent, I'm sure very little meaningful parenting is done between working, providing for children's basic necessities, and sleeping. So many parents are doing the job of two and barely hanging on themselves that most of the time all they want is a little peace. So if that means sitting the kid in front of the TV while mama has a cocktail, or letting preteens keep the computers in their rooms because at least they're out of your face for a minute, or letting teenagers come and go as they please because you are tired of the fighting (plus you are trying to go out and have a good time your damn self), then so be it.

There is no doubt that our community can prevail and take back our families. However, the first step is acknowledging that these issues do exist. Life is not a parent–teacher conference. We must stop acting like our kids are so damn perfect all the time. The first step in taking back control of our children is admitting we have lost it.

The stakes are high. What bad parents fail to realize is that when they perform poorly as parents, their kids become everyone else's problem. I got 99 problems, and your kid shouldn't be one of them. Life is complicated enough without me having to worry about little Jamal and LaShanta beating me about the head as I walk home from the bus stop.

You have to approach parenting in terms of front-end and back-end decisions. On the front end, you need to make better decisions about if and when and with whom you have these children:

❑ Stop meeting people at the club and five weeks later discovering that you are pregnant with their child.

❑ Stop having children with men who you know already have kids they are not supporting.

❑ Plan your pregnancies. Children should be a planned decision between two people who are committed to raising them together.

Before you think about having children, your first step should be getting a husband or wife. A 2005 report by the Institute for American Values, a nonpartisan group that studies the sociology of families, showed that "economically, marriage for black Americans is a wealth-creating and poverty-reducing institution. The marital status of African American parents is one of the most powerful determinants of the economic status of African American families." Thirty-five percent of black women who have a child out of wedlock live in poverty; only 17 percent of married black women live in poverty.

Marital status also plays a role in the future of the children. It is well documented that children from single-parent homes are more likely to drop out of school, be arrested, and have children out of wedlock themselves. A 1999 University of Chicago study found that 78 percent of the nation's jail and prison inmates grew up in fatherless households. It goes on to state that adults who grew up fatherless are 20 times more likely to be imprisoned than adults who grew up with a father present.

In 2008, during his presidential campaign, President Obama, who knows firsthand how it feels to grow up without a dad, addressed this problem in a speech given at a church on Father's Day. He acknowledged that 50 percent of our children live in single-parent households and stated that although fatherless homes are a problem everywhere, "nowhere is it more glaring than in the black community." He went on to say that "too many fathers are missing from too many lives and too many homes; they've abandoned their responsibilities . . . and the foundations of our families have suffered because of it."

Many men have let down our communities. Too many men have children all over town and don't support any of them. And a check is not support. Children need their fathers to be there. To read to them and play games with them and listen to them and teach them to be young men and women. They don't need your $75 a week as much as they need you to be there when there's a thunderstorm or when they win their first science fair award (those erupting papier-mâché volcanoes win every time). Support isn't just the money the government takes out of your check. It's being there for the nightmares and skinned knees and puppy love and bike rides. Don't lament how much child support you are paying; rejoice in how much time you are spending with your children. Unfortunately, too many men simply walk away from their responsibilities and never look back. There is a special place in Hades for them.

And although many women complain nonstop about their children's fathers not being in their lives, I am here to say that there is also a huge problem with women keeping their children away from their dads and using them as pawns in petty games. If you withhold a child from his or her father because of financial reasons, because you and the dad don't get along, or because you have moved on to yet another relationship, then you are guilty of short-changing that child out of a father. I have witnessed mothers who will walk through fire to minimize the time their children spend with their fathers because of petty personal issues they have with their exes.

Of course, it's outrageous if a man doesn't support his children financially, but financial support isn't a way to buy time with them. Fathers should spend time with their children regardless of child support disputes. To withhold a child from his or her father because of your own spite, anger, money issues, or bitterness is only punishing the child, who deserves all the love he or she can get.

Look, ladies, you may not need a man, but your child needs a father. How can you show your children what a healthy relationship looks like if they've never seen one? How can you teach your kids how a man is supposed to treat a woman when they have never seen a man in your home for more than a few nights? This strategy is just not working. So you may want to think twice about your whole, "I don't need a man to raise my child; I can be a mother and father" crap. YOU CAN'T.

But let's back up a little and talk about something that too few people think about. Decide if you even WANT children. Having children should be a conscious choice, not a default. Find your life's passion or a hobby or, God forbid, go to a gym, and then maybe you won't have to have kids just to fill the hole in your soul.

(Quick confession: sometimes when I am experiencing overwhelming angst and I can't quite figure out what I want to do with my life or what steps to take next, I think, *Maybe I'll just have a baby*. When I can't quite figure out what will make me happy, I say to myself, *Well, I'll just have a baby—I'm sure that will make me happy*. And then I wake up and realize what a trick my mind and heart are playing on me. It's a lazy cop-out move. I'm thinking about me, not that child. I wonder how many women have fallen prey to the baby = happiness myth? No, a happy woman = happiness [baby or not].)

Next, I know it sounds crazy, but birth control, birth control, birth control. Unless you're the Virgin Mary, pregnancy is not something that just happens.

- PLAN to have children. They should not be had by default, because you're getting older, because you were too lazy or drunk to use birth control, to keep a man, or because you simply are filling some hole in your own soul.

- Don't have children with losers.

There is no excuse for "mistakes." If you don't want a child, science has seen to it that you don't have to have one. It kills me to hear Bristol Palin—daughter of Sarah Palin, the 2008 Republican vice-presidential nominee—say that if she could wave a magic wand she would have waited another 10 years before she had a baby. *Newsflash:* you don't need a magic wand; it's called contraception. We act like we have no role and no responsibility in unplanned pregnancies. We do.

If you have a child and are already struggling, maybe another baby is not what you need right now. I've never understood why people who were already broke and barely getting by decide to have more children. Your most important gift to a child is your time. If you are dividing your waking hours between two or three jobs and two or three children, the kids are the ones who will ultimately suffer.

I know you love children and think you got pregnant because God wanted you to and all that bullshit, but get real. The only way it's excusable to be poor and have five kids nowadays is if you live in a polygamist compound or if you are the Octomom. Stop bringing children that you can't care for into the world. You are taking away their chances at success before they can even talk. You are making their lives miserable and making yourself miserable to boot because you won't think past the oohs and ahs of new little baby Jordans. If you really love children, you would make sure you are bringing them into an environment that will nurture them, support them, and allow them to reach their full potential. If you don't have the ability to do that, please don't have any more kids.

I know most of these front-end directives are aimed at women, but truth be told, women are ultimately responsible for their own bodies and their own decisions. I'm just bringing common sense back. There are so many decisions we make that have a permanent and irreversibly negative impact on our quality of life and that of the children we bring into the world. If we just stop for a split second and *think* about the consequences certain decisions will have, our quality of life will improve exponentially.

But let's just assume you've skimmed the above paragraphs, and now you find yourself with kids, with or without a mate. The deed is done, and little Renee or Malcolm is here. Time to face parenting from the back end.

Now that you have them, it is up to you, moms and dads, to raise your children, set high expectations for them, teach them to be responsible for their actions, and love them to pieces. Bill Cosby wrote in an op-ed piece published in the *Los Angeles Times* in 2004, "What we need now is more parents sitting down with their children, overseeing homework, sending children off to school in the morning well fed, clothed and ready to learn." Think about that list for a moment; is this how you live your life with your kids? If no, then why not?

When it comes down to it, these basic steps can go such a long way. It's so simple it almost feels ridiculous saying this to adults. But, of course, it only sounds simple. Raising children is actually a full-time job and a lot of hard work for active, involved parents. But you brought them here, so now that they're here, raise them right. Why do parents need to be reminded to be parents? Not BFs, not shopping buddies, not club partners.

There are no other options. And sure, I have a vested interest in your doing all these things, because if you raise your kids right, it is less likely that I will get my iPod and cell phone snatched as I walk to the corner store for some beef franks.

Unfortunately, judging by what I see on the streets every day, many parents are failing miserably at this admittedly simple charge. One need only look at the current condition of our schools, the high dropout rates, and the juvenile incarceration rates, to know that kids are out of control, everywhere. Hell, one needs only to walk down the street or take public transportation in the afternoons. David Nicholson wrote in the *Washington Post*, "Did all those who suffered and died for freedom, all the martyrs of the civil rights movement such as Medgar Evers . . . and Martin Luther King Jr. really give their lives so that a generation of young blacks could act out in public as if they were characters in a gangster movie or rap song?" We have simply come too far and worked too hard to turn our streets over to problem children that we were responsible for creating.

This summer a dear friend of mine decided to take his MBA degree from Wharton Business School and begin a mentoring program for young people in the D.C. area. He partnered with another Wharton grad to work with teenagers on career development. He wanted to give urban youth a broader vision for the possibilities in their lives and then teach them how to make goals and create a plan to achieve them. So here you have two outstanding business minds who could have chosen to go any-where from Wall Street to the Silicon Valley, instead working with these young people. Kudos to them!

He would talk in the evenings about his daily experiences with these kids, and I was shocked to see his transformation from hopeful and optimistic to disenchanted, frustrated, and utterly at his wits' end with regard to these kids. It reminded me of a *Frontline* episode on the Teach for America program. After three months, those newbie teachers looked like they all had post-traumatic stress disorder. Well, my friend who had started his program with high hopes was amazed at the levels of dis-respect and laziness and the sense of entitlement these kids exhibited. He had to kick several kids out of the program because they refused to follow simple rules. They would show up late, talk back to instruc-tors, constantly complain, leave class in the middle of the day, and God knows what else.

One weekend, he arranged for his kids to attend a conference on entrepreneurship where they would get to work with high-achieving stu-dents from all over the country. They would get to stay in a college dorm and have a new and exciting experience on a college campus. Three young men were sent home the first day for skipping the workshops. The next day, three young women missed their workshops because, in their words (spoken indignantly, I might add), they're not used to get-ting up before 10:00 A.M. on a Saturday. Did I mention these kids were getting paid to attend?

Now, these were not stupid kids. They were intelligent and had the potential to do well but just didn't have any work ethic, gratitude, respect for education, or personal accountability. They had never been taught these things. When confronted with their children's bad behavior, the parents would make excuses for their kids and tell the heads of the program that they were being too harsh. Instead of challenging their children's behavior, they immediately attacked the instructors. Forget that their kids broke the rules; it's the rules' fault—they're too strict.

And in five years everyone will wonder why these kids can't hold on to a job. How do young people learn responsibility and consequences when parents make excuses for them? How do they learn excellence when we don't require it of them?

In the end, my do-gooder friend decided that, the following year, he would enact stricter requirements in order to screen out disruptive students. He said that the 80 percent of students who came to class and acted a fool held back the 20 percent who actually wanted to learn something. He loved to work with young people, but he wanted to work with kids who *wanted* to succeed and excel. He didn't have time to beg students to improve themselves and learn something. Teaching kids ambition and the pursuit of excellence is their parents' job. He was there to teach them how to achieve their goals once they set them.

That's probably the biggest complaint I hear from my teacher-friends. There just isn't enough time in the day to effectively teach kids academics while simultaneously dealing with 20 behavioral problems in a class of 24. There are so many talented teachers who leave the field because they have been reduced to day-care providers, spending the bulk of their time trying to teach kids how to act (something that should have been taught at home). You can't neglect your duties as a parent for 15 years and then expect a teacher to clean up your mess.

I have friends who come home complaining that they couldn't PAY parents to come to a parent-teacher conference. But if little Tony does something wrong and gets into trouble, the same parents are ready to come up to the school, defend little Tony, and cuss everybody else out. One male friend who is a teacher was called a faggot by one of his elementary-school students. Instead of apologizing to the teacher for his child's offensive behavior, the kid's father wanted to fight him. There were also two recent incidents at a local high school where parents actually did get into physical fights! If the parents are acting a fool, what hope do the kids have? The lunatics are running the asylum.

The parents who claim that everyone is at fault but them and their children do their children such a disservice. This method does not prepare them for the real world where they will be held wholly responsible for the decisions they make. How will they learn about consequences if we never hold them accountable for their behavior? The answer? They won't.

Kids that grow up with no accountability usually end up in my law office 10 years later, trying to get out of paying their rent. They are now age 25, with two kids by two different people, and have had three jobs in six months. Every single job resulted in a termination. But, of course, it was never their fault. Their bosses just didn't like them, or they believed they were fired because they were black. Or they got fired for being late every day, but it wasn't fair because their busses were always late, so it wasn't their fault.

We are raising a generation of eternal babies who aren't able to accept responsibility for their lives. We have stopped requiring it. They only know crying and whining. Mamas, don't let your babies grow up to be pathetic.

- ❑ Listen to parents, teachers, and other adults who tell you that your child is a badass. They're usually right.

- ❑ Don't make excuses for your kids. They should be held accountable for their behavior.

- ❑ Making excuses and "taking their side" only turns kids into men and women who make excuses for themselves and never accept responsibility for their actions.

JAM THE NEGRO

You know it would take some uppity Negro without kids to sit here and talk about how everyone else should raise theirs. That's right—blame everything on the parents. You probably support those laws that put parents in jail for what their kids do. As a parent, you only have so much control over your kids once they walk out of the door. You can't monitor them 24 hours a day. By the time you get home from work, all you can do is get dinner on the table and make sure they get to bed. I am not a Superwoman. Just like that song. And why are you all up in my uterus trying to tell me who I should and should not have kids with? Children are a blessing from God, and I don't care how you get pregnant or by whom, why should that child pay the price? I don't have to be married with a white picket fence to raise my kids right. And, hell yes, I challenge those teachers, because half of them don't know what they are doing and take it out on the kids. They are not going to make my child a scapegoat simply because they can't get control of their classes. And as far as the kids being motivated, it's the school system's fault. The buildings are dilapidated, the teachers are terrible, and they barely have books. How does anyone expect a child to learn in an environment like that? But see, no one wants to talk about that. No one wants to talk about how the government doesn't care about inner-city children. They want our kids to fail. The government closed all the recreation centers so the kids have nothing to do after school but get into trouble. When it comes to kids in the inner city, all they care about is putting in metal detectors. Stop being so overdramatic, talking about how our kids are not prepared for the future. Our kids will be just fine. News-flash: you don't have to go to college to be successful. Plenty of successful people like Jay-Z and Diddy and Beyoncé never went to college. College isn't for everyone. Maybe once you experience having kids and raising them in the city, I'll listen to what you have to say.

JAM THE AMERICAN ⭐

If I hear one more person say "college isn't for everyone," I'm gonna scream. How will you know if it's for you or not if you don't go? We are fooling ourselves if we think that we can keep allowing our kids to slide by in this day and age. College is not only important, it's absolutely necessary. I was recently speaking to a group of 11th and 12th graders, none of whom had even considered filling out a college application. Where are the parents in this process? Sure, the schools are a disaster, but where the schools fall short, it is a parent's responsibility to fill in the gaps. If your guidance counselor doesn't recommend college, then your mama should be the one requesting applications for you. Inner-city schools have always been a mess, but even with a substandard school system, when parents and dedicated teachers are involved, students can still thrive. It's first and foremost about instilling in children the importance of getting an education. I never even knew college was optional. My parents spoke of it like it was the 13th grade, something you automatically did after 12th grade. Kids these days couldn't care less about getting an education, and the parents aren't telling them any different.

And for the record, all kids aren't gifts from God. Some babies are gifts from tequila shots. That's why God invented birth control. I hear women loudly proclaim they don't need a man—well, maybe not, BUT THE KID NEEDS A FATHER. It's so selfish to sentence a child to life without a father's love because you want to be sexually irresponsible and act out on some misplaced feminist bullshit. At the same time, so many fathers of this generation have been pathetic excuses for men. It's really an outrage. Men that ran from the KKK now run from their own kids. Don't you know that most of the young people in jail right now grew up without fathers? Do you think this is some coincidence? Children need involved dads. I am so sick of dealing with your badass fatherless children. They are loud, disrespectful, and don't have any home training.

And no, the teachers don't care. After dealing with your spawns of Satan for three years, I probably wouldn't care either. Plus, it's not the teacher's job to teach your kids how to act. It's your job. It's your job to teach your children how to be young men and women. Stop blaming everyone but yourselves for the bad shape our kids are in. When was the last time you went over their homework with them? When was the last time you sat and worked with your son on his reading? When was the last time you took your kids to a museum? When was the last time you cut off the TV and took their fat asses around the block for a walk?

I always hear, "They closed all the rec centers and that's why the kids are getting into trouble." What a crock. I don't think I went to a rec center *once* growing up, but my alternative activity was not stealing cars. There are many opportunities available to supplement and enhance your children's education and development if you just take the time to find them. It's hard work, but it is your duty to prepare them as best you can for this cold, cruel world. Because right now, they have someone who cares about them—you. Soon they'll be grown and no one will give a shit that they are broke, have no skills, and can't hold a job. And if you don't have the time to raise your children right, perhaps you shouldn't have any more. Because they grow up and become everyone's problem.

Of course, not all kids are all bad. I have seen many young people grow and thrive. I met a young man who had lost both of his parents to drugs and jail and was now staying with an aunt and uncle. His intelligence, manners, positive outlook, and perseverance inspire everyone who meets him. I met some young people who have learned to sew and started their own business selling clothes and handbags. They are phenomenal! My young cousin has defied the odds and enrolled in college. Everywhere you find examples of kids excelling, you will generally find adults in close proximity who refused to lose their kids to the streets or, maybe worse, mediocrity.

We just have to make sure these are the kids that we hold up as examples, these are the kids we praise and reward. It is our job to make sure they never lose that spark in their eyes. We must give all of our kids constant reinforcement and encouragement. Assure them that dumb is not cool. Failing is not fly. It amazes me how adults will use positive reinforcement techniques to train their dogs but not use them to mold their kids.

That leads me to the It Takes a Village/Damned If You Do, Damned If You Don't paradox. Don't think this is just about the kids. I figure this mess has two culpable parties: parents and village elders (people who don't have children but have to deal with everyone else's). So now that I've lambasted the parents, let's get to the rest of the village, the elders, like me. A part of the problem, and likely the main part, is that we adults see all this going on and don't do a damn thing about it. Just like those kids I heard singing on the street. I didn't stop, chastise them, and tell them that they should be ashamed of themselves, that they are bringing shame to their family, or that I was going to tell their daddy on them. I just kept walking, shaking my head, being disgusted. Ultimately, though, like the passengers on buses and subways every day, I did nothing.

If it takes a village to raise a child, yet the village is afraid or indifferent, then aren't we fooling ourselves? Why aren't the village elders more vested in mentoring and helping out this next generation?

On the other hand, I can't be too hard on the village elders because, the first time you attempt to correct a village child, the village mama is likely gonna beat your village ass. So what do you do? The days of rebuking other people's children are gone. You can't even tell a child to hush without getting cussed out by Big Mama. You can't confront a child in any way without fear of getting beat down and ending up as a YouTube video clip of the day. So many of us don't care, and those who do care are afraid to act. Like me. So where does that leave us?

In the crapper. Much like my friend who ran the summer program, our lives are too complicated to invest excess energy in raising other people's children. Isn't it ironic that everyone seems too busy to do the most important job in the world? The task becomes even more daunting when you feel neither the child nor parent will appreciate it anyway.

Consequently, the well-behaved, motivated, disciplined children will begin to move farther and farther from the rest of the pack, creating a children's version of the have/have-not dichotomy. Those who CAN volunteer their time and energy won't want to waste them just trying to get kids to shut up for five minutes. Problem kids and underachievers will be ditched, and the attention will be focused on those who want to learn, are willing to follow the rules, and are motivated to succeed. In the end, all the resources will be focused on those who probably have the best chances for success any-

❑ **Set high standards for young people and hold them accountable for meeting them.**

❑ **Having low standards only sabotages your children and encourages mediocrity.**

❑ **Reward achievement. Positive reinforcement for excellence will pay off in spades.**

way, while the rest of the pack and their parents will be left behind, creating a permanent, growing, and scary underclass.

What is most frightening about the state of our young people and their prospects for the future is that there is simply no longer a place for unmotivated underachievers barely making it out of high school. Back in the day, maybe these slackers could make a decent living in manufacturing or low-grade government employment or at the post office. But as automation reduces the need for many of these jobs and the manufacturing industry in this country becomes a thing of the past, where does this crew go? They are being outpaced by technology and being outworked by immigrants. The world is literally passing them by.

So it becomes not only a moral imperative to address these young people, but also an economic one. What are the negative economic implications for a growing underclass? We must ensure our country is competitive in a global economy, or we're doomed. People are now resorting to paying kids to go to school or creating sophisticated incentive programs to foster academic achievement? It's almost funny. My only incentive growing up was, "Don't get a C or you'll be punished." Those were the days. Alas, it is a different age. Hard work is no longer in vogue.

There was a time when our young people had so many dreams, so much vision, but very little opportunity. Now the opportunities are there, but the vision and dreams have dried up like raisins in the sun. I want a world where parents stress education, instill in their children a sense of greatness, demand respect for themselves and all other adults, teach responsibility and accountability, and, most importantly, act as their children's biggest advocates.

I wish I knew how to make this happen. I wish I had some $64,000 answer that would result in a highly motivated, eager-to-learn, reach-for-the-stars generation. However, I don't. I think I'm just as confused as everyone else. I fear for our future. I am scared that too many young people will look up in 10 years and have no place to go. No skills, no work ethic, no vision, no motivation, and, worst of all, no responsibility for how they ended up there in the first place.

For now, I exist in that odd place where I am simultaneously inspired, disgusted, fearful, frustrated, and proud of our young people. I just wish more parents stressed the importance of education and excellence. I wish there were fewer excuses and more accountability. I wish more parents were better examples to their children. I wish more children grew up with two involved parents. I wish there were more hard work and less getting by. I wish there were more gratitude and less entitlement. I wish children grew up knowing that the world is ripe with opportunity and that the possibilities for their lives are limitless.

But then again, I also wish I weighed 125 pounds and that my boobs were perkier. So what can you do?

7

"GHETTO FABULOUS"
IS AN OXYMORON

"Everything costs a lot of money when you haven't got any."

—*Joe Louis*

Brand-new, limited-edition Louis Vuitton bag: $1,500. Mercedes CLK 420: $600 per month. Malaysian human-hair weave: $800. *No college fund for your kids*: senseless.

Now, I have been known to fuck up some money in my day. I spend too much eating and drinking out, too much on entertaining myself and friends, too much on sarcastic and profane T-shirts. I have more debt than I should and often splurge on waxing and massages and electronic gizmos I don't use. Believe me, I'm no Suze Orman.

But I manage to pay my bills, keep some money in the bank, have an IRA, and basically get it done. The one thing that has probably saved me from financial ruin is knowing how to set priorities. And not having kids.

Just joking.

But not really.

I am very fortunate to have grown up with financially prudent parents who, from my very first allowance of five dollars a week, always instilled in me the importance of saving. I was taught in high school about bank accounts and credit and stocks and mutual funds. I was told never to cash a check. Don't get me wrong—my parents didn't have a lot of money. But the money they had was used wisely and saved religiously. I always had a job and, with my parents' words echoing in my ears, have never cashed a check in my life.

Then, of course, you go to college and discover credit cards. You soon rack up massive debt, get dozens of parking tickets, and loan money to trifling men you thought you loved, both of which are soon gone. I know; I was guilty of it all. College teaches us lots of things, little of which is taught in the classroom. We learn important lessons about love, life, sex, and, of course, money.

Those of us who aren't trust-fund babies are forced to become master budgeters. We must figure out how many cups of Ramen noodles and how many grilled cheese sandwiches, condoms, and cases of beer we can get out of that last $20.

College often reveals what type of money manager you will be. I always paid my bills, even if it was the minimum payment possible. I just felt like a loser if I owed money and didn't pay—I just felt guilty about it. And I'm not even Catholic. Call it good training, but I always thought the responsible thing was to pay your bills no matter how long it took. Sure, the debt was for totally worthless things, but it was mine, and I just had that bill-paying instinct.

However, most of my friends did not. Many of my friends had absolutely no qualms about walking away from bills or other financial obligations. They would just toss the monthly statements in the trash and keep it moving. They soon learned, as with most bad decisions we make, financial irresponsibility eventually comes back to haunt you.

By age 21, whether you've been to college or not, you should understand the importance of things like credit scores, budgeting, saving, and
paying bills on time. At some point, whether you want to or not, you
become an adult. Unfortunately, too many of us are not growing up
financially.

Excessive consumerism and an obsession with bling are certainly
not confined to any particular demographic. We are a nation of excess
and instant gratification. It has become the American way. We are a
buy-it-now-pay-for-it-later nation. However, as more and more of our
value seems to be attached to stuff, the toll materialism is taking on
the African American population—which generally has less savings,
lower rates of home ownership, and less generational wealth—is enormous. Enormous in the straight dollars-and-cents way, sure; but it is
also taking a toll on our priorities, goals, and our concepts of success.
Too many are sacrificing their future security for a long weave and a
plastic VIP armband.

The element of sacrifice has been removed from the concept of
wealth. To many people, wealth is an overnight gift showered down upon
you from the heavens. Many young people no longer equate hard work
with money. Hard work is for suckas. We are bombarded with images of
young, beautiful people who live in fabulous houses and drive fabulous
cars and who sun themselves on the shores of fabulous beaches. It looks
so easy. We aim to emulate these people.

But that's like all those young white girls trying to look like the air-
brushed models in magazines. They are chasing a dream. Idolizing a
fantasy. Obsessed with the pursuit of something that does not exist. We
don't see the sacrifice and hard work that came before the success, and
we don't see the tens of thousands who never made it that far.

When you ask young people what they want to be when they grow
up, the decades-old standard response of "doctor or lawyer" has now
been replaced with "entertainer or athlete." They don't necessarily want
to *do* anything in particular. They just know they want to be rich.

But rich is not a career. Many a teenager's sole life goal is to replicate the lifestyles of people who, in many instances, are dead broke. I recently asked a 10-year-old boy what he wanted to be when he grew up.

He replied, "Football player."

I said, "If you couldn't be a football player, what would you be?"

He said, "Basketball player."

I said, "What if you couldn't be a basketball player?"

He replied, "A baseball player."

We're doomed.

And it's not just the young people who think this way. I was watching one of those god-awful reality shows that involves contestants competing for an opportunity to work for a successful celebrity mogul. The show begins with the various candidates explaining why they want to work for this person. One guy said that from the time he was a child, he knew he wanted to be rich. He didn't know how he was going to do it, but he wanted to be rich.

And everyone's aspirations were similar in that regard. They wanted to be successful, and working for a celebrity would open doors for them. Sure, these reasons sound very benign on the surface, but on closer examination, their logic reveals a major flaw that has developed in the American dream.

None of the candidates had a particular *career* they were interested in. None of them had their eyes on a special position. None of them had been working since an early age toward a specific goal. They didn't see this show as a stepping stone on a path toward their aspirations. The show *was* their aspiration.

> ❑ **Rich is not a career. Figure out your passion and plan your career goals. Then act earnestly to achieve them.**

These folks saw this show as a shortcut on the road to success. We're living in this *American Idol* paradigm. Forget working hard, setting goals, and planning out a path for our lives. We've reduced success to a big break, to that one thing that comes along and changes everything.

I also hear many young people who, when asked what they want to do with their lives, respond, "I want to be in the entertainment business." What in the sam hill does that mean? "I want to be a mogul and own a lot of companies"? Or maybe just, "I want to be rich." Yet, when pressed about specifics, they have no clue what they want or how they're going to get it.

Being a multimedia mogul is a fantastic goal. However, regardless of what it may seem like on TV, it does not just happen. You don't win a successful career on a show. You don't stumble upon it. It doesn't happen by accident. So many believe success is something that will simply fall into their laps when the stars align. And for that reason, young people grow up with dreams but no plan. You can't achieve your dreams without a plan.

You rarely hear someone say, "I plan to go to college, get an MBA, then start my own company managing talent." THAT'S a goal; that's a career; that's a plan. To use a sports analogy, you have to move TO the ball; you can't just wait for it.

Now, don't get me wrong—many of us aren't quite sure what we want to do and there's nothing wrong with that. I certainly took a long time finding myself, and I don't know if I've found me yet (and, believe me, I've looked everywhere). However, I positioned myself so when I did finally decide what I wanted to do, I would be well prepared. Education is the key to excelling, no matter what field you want to enter. And it doesn't have to be higher education. Having an apprenticeship or internship, taking a continuing education class, or simply a working with a mentor can set the stage for entering a career with something more than just dreams of success.

To put it another way, although I'm still waiting for Denzel Washington to sweep me off my feet, I signed up for eHarmony just in case. Get it?

You can't work toward a goal if you don't have one. Being rich is not a goal, although achieving your goals can result in making you very rich. Many folks just don't seem to get that nuance. We spend more time positioning ourselves for the sudden break than we do getting educated, interning, learning the field, working hard, and paying dues. Dues? This generation has no concept of dues.

We idolize the rich and famous. Our children dream of being Diddy or Beyoncé. What they don't understand, because we don't teach them, is that Diddy, as annoying a narcissist as he may be, paid his dues. He started as an intern and worked his way up, learning the business inside out. As sickeningly perfect as Beyoncé is, she had to bust her ass on the chitlin circuit and work extremely hard for a long time before she made it. There was no *American Idol* to ensure instant fame; there was no reality show to make them stars out of thin air.

We are so inundated with this Soulja Boy/reality TV paradigm of success that we forget how most of the people at the very top really got there: by knowing what they wanted and working their asses off to get it.

So the next time you are speaking to a young person about goals, and he or she says something like "I want to be in the entertainment industry," ask what that means. "Do you want to be a costume designer, an actress, a makeup artist, a director of photography, a stylist, a set designer, an agent, A&R, or what?"

Next time you hear, "I want to be a mogul," ask, "Well, what does that mean exactly, and what are you doing to train yourself to enter the business world?"

Next time you hear, "I just want to be rich," ask, "How do you plan on getting rich and what steps are you taking toward that plan?" Being on *Cribs* is not a career plan; designing them is. You can't work toward a goal if you don't have one.

Only when you identify a field, position, or career you are interested in can you start to design and implement a plan for your life. There's nothing wrong with dreaming. But dreams coupled with inaction virtually guarantee that your dreams will remain just that. Dreams.

And when all you have are dreams and no plan, you begin to do things to substitute for those dreams coming true. Like buying a house you can't afford, like racking up credit card debt. If you haven't actually realized all those dreams, at least you can look like you have. A big house and fancy cars should not be goals; they should be the result of you having reached your goals.

It seems both parents and kids alike want the same things. In fact, our lives have become constant quests to acquire *things*. We don't search for security, integrity, or quality—just things. And it shows. It shows in the way many of us live our lives. Forget trying to do well—we just need to *look* like we're doing well.

This focus on stuff and appearances is killing us. It seems that our communities have discarded basic common sense with regard to how we manage our finances. We put so much focus on things that ultimately depreciate. Cars, clothes, jewelry, electronics, and hair care suck up an enormous amount of black wealth. Wealth that the community never sees again.

However, there are bright lights of financial responsibility all over— you just have to look a little harder for them. I have a dear friend who pinched and scraped and sacrificed so he could graduate from law school absolutely debt free. I have a friend whose mom never had the latest technology—she still has a rotary dial phone on the wall. But she was able to pay off her home and retire at 50 from a modest-paying government job simply because she was a fierce saver. My best friend refuses to buy new clothes and always shops at consignment stores and thrift shops and pays her credit card off every month. There are certainly financially responsible citizens who are holding it down. However, too often these are the exceptions and not the rule.

Parents are setting bad financial examples for their children. Children are wearing clothes that are more expensive than mine. They are living in a house that their parents can't afford and riding in an SUV whose gas bill is more than monthly groceries. They don't see restraint; they don't see sacrifice and saving. The parents are too busy keeping up with the Joneses and the Joneses' kids.

Perhaps there is more at work here. With the prevalence of single-parent households in the black community, we often replace the time we cannot spend with children with gifts. Parents assuage their guilt by indulging the child. We expect less of them and give them more. Soon we have a generation who expects to get everything they want without doing anything in return. But then they become adults and expect to maintain the same lifestyles. So what do they do but spend recklessly, rack up debt on their own credit cards, then drown in debt? And then the cycle begins again. We are going to spend away the economic gains of the last 50 years.

Kids should learn at home about saving, delayed gratification, retirement, and the importance of good credit. We can help our kids avoid the pitfalls we faced by speaking openly about money and setting responsible examples. Sometimes that may mean breaking some long-held traditions and bad habits.

> ❑ Connect money and gifts with achievement or hard work like good grades or household chores. Children must learn the relationship between work and money early in life.

There are certain financial behaviors that have been passed down through the generations. They are part of our amazing history in this country and should be revered as examples of our ingenuity and will to survive in the face of slavery, Jim Crow, disenfranchisement, and segregation. However, times have changed, and it's time for some of our money habits to change too.

For one, this lottery shit has got to go. I know your grandma and your great-grandma both ran numbers and that's how you got your prom dress, but those days are over. It never ceases to amaze me how much money people spend on the lottery. My neighborhood has a couple of liquor stores, and when I go in to buy, uhhhh, "potato chips," the lottery line is often to the back of the store. And these folks are not buying just one lottery ticket. There are people there who play more than $20 a day. I once saw a woman buy $60 worth of scratch-off tickets. I wanted to ask her, *Really?*

Now sure, one will say, these people are poor and desperate and see the lottery as their only means to escape poverty. However, it just makes no damn sense. You want to escape poverty by pissing up money? To many of us, it's just a habit. It's something we do because it's something we've always done. Our parents played, our grandparents played, our neighbors play, and soon you have your own favorite number, a dream book, and you're going into the store with one of those long pieces of paper outlining a betting system as sophisticated as uranium enrichment.

But do me a favor: next time you're in the store buying lottery tickets, look around you and notice how EVERYONE LOOKS BROKE. Then look in a mirror. Avid lottery players, just think how much money you would have if you put those same funds in an interest-bearing account for your retirement or a college fund. We have to play the game smarter, and eliminating the lottery as a retirement plan is such an easy way to keep money in the hands of our most vulnerable citizens. But no one is going to make you spend your money more wisely. Our money is our responsibility. I don't care if there is a Keno machine and lottery store on every corner, we must take responsibility for the choices we make with our finances. The lottery is a no-brainer, people.

Another cultural tradition that has limited economic growth for many of us is this fear of banking. What's that about? I know so many people who say they don't trust banks. "I don't know what they're gonna do with my money," they say. They opt instead for a life of check cashing and money orders. So instead of getting 3 percent interest on your money paid by a bank, you'd rather pay the check cashing store 3 percent for access to your own money? How do we justify this?

When you deposit money in a bank, much like your car or Tina Turner's legs, it is insured. The Federal Deposit Insurance Corporation (FDIC) insures all deposits up to $100,000. So this pervasive fear of losing the money you deposit in a bank is a misguided urban legend that, in the end, costs us big.

Unless you're an illegal immigrant or a felon or you owe a bank some money, you have no business using check cashing places. As my great-grandmother would say, "That's money right up the cat's ass."

We must be accountable for our decisions about how we spend and manage money in our communities. I always hear, "Well, they put lottery tickets, furniture rental stores, and check cashing places in black neighborhoods to exploit minorities." Maybe it's because our dumb asses continue to go. You can't simultaneously accuse a business of taking advantage of you and then continue to patronize it. That's idiocy. If it doesn't make dollars, it doesn't make sense.

We must be smarter. So your mama did not have a banking account and maybe your daddy didn't either. Wake up. You know better now. So it's time to do better. You have information and opportunities other generations did not. Make an assessment of your financial condition and research what options for money management are open to you. If you want to be a big baller, first act like one and make managing your funds a priority. Don't let bad habits of the past continue to hold you back. Don't participate in your own exploitation and then complain. Only you determine how you spend your money.

At the other end of the financial spectrum, growing numbers of African Americans are excelling in education and in the work force and accumulating substantial wealth. And while acquiring wealth is a great thing, we must be very careful what we do with it. Because most of us do not come from long lines of generational wealth, sometimes we have not been taught about managing money in a way that will guarantee a life of security for ourselves and our children. Like most Americans, we spend way too much in an attempt to let everyone know we have arrived. But it's specifically what we spend our money on that is so disturbing.

We tend to focus on things that depreciate instead of things that appreciate. We have a passionate love affair with cars, clothes, rims, and jewelry. Just because you heard a designer mentioned on *Sex and the City* or in a rap song doesn't mean you have to run out and buy his or her products. I know women who, at 30, are filing for bankruptcy because they got addicted to the lifestyle of the rich and famous, without actually being rich or famous. You can party like a rap star, just don't end up broke like most of them.

We spend an inordinate amount of money buying expensive cognac and purses, renting VIP tables, and getting $1,000 hair weaves. Now all that is nice, and I believe if you work hard you deserve to reward yourself, but just make sure you have a house, a computer, an IRA, and a college fund first.

We tend to be short-sighted with our money. We lull ourselves into believing that the money well will never run dry and the good times will never end. This stops us from planning for the day when the checks are not coming in. What if you get laid off? What if you become disabled? Do

> ❑ **Stop spending so much money on a bunch of depreciating bullshit. Clothes, cars, jewelry, weaves, and shoes all depreciate. See what $1,200 invested in a mutual fund will be worth in 10 years as opposed to those hot pink Manolo Blahniks.**

you have life insurance, long-term care insurance, disability insurance? Shouldn't you? It is vital that we plan our lives as carefully as we plan our outfits. Contribute the max to your 401(k), stop spending more than you make, and don't borrow from your retirement account for that Bermuda trip. Achieving financial security takes planning and discipline. Joe Louis, the great boxer, once famously said, "Everything costs a lot of money when you haven't got any."

JAM THE NEGRO

My financial plan: reparations now! I find it really amazing how everyone in this country got rich off the black man, except the black man. How do you think these wealthy families got their money? Slavery! But no one wants to talk about that. So their legacy is wealth and our legacy is poverty? And now we're just supposed to go on like nothing ever happened? They deprive us of our 40 acres and a mule and we're just supposed to be good little Negroes and get over it? I don't think so. I'm not gonna play into this corrupt and racist financial system that was built on the blood of my ancestors. I don't know when these delusional middle-class blacks are going to realize that the white system of oppression that we currently live under will never let the black race become financially self-sufficient. That's why they place these parasitic businesses in our communities—to keep us broke. To hell with a bank. They just get all in your business and gather a bunch of data on you so they can keep track of what you're doing. These misguided black people think that if you just play the game, you can get ahead. Don't they know that the game isn't meant for us? It never was. So you may as well have fun while you can. It doesn't matter what we do, because we'll never get ahead. They keep us broke and then put us in jail when we are just trying to survive the streets they have relegated us to. It's a gimmick. An illusion. The AmeriKKKan dream is a nightmare for black people, and I refuse to buy into this pie-in-the-sky bullshit. If you think that all we have to do is work hard and save money and we can thrive in this country, then I guess the brainwashing has really worked. Free Mumia!

JAM THE AMERICAN

You can talk about racism until your mouth catches on fire, but there is no way that you will make me believe that black folks don't have the opportunity to thrive. It's about taking advantage of it. I live in an urban area and I don't see Mr. Charlie herding black people into the lottery line. I don't see the Grand Wizard taking black folks to go buy cars they can't afford. Is Chez Whitey the reason you don't have a will? Did the Cracka Man make you max out five credit cards on God knows what, all the while you still don't have a college fund for your children? I guess that was his fault too. But it's cool, while you and your ilk cry and whine and beg for a reparations check, I'm going to handle my business. I'm going to get educated, work hard, and pay my dues. I will be professional and manage my money well. I will provide a plan for my life and one for my death. So you can waste your time and sit around talking about what you don't have and whose fault it is if you want to. Have you ever heard of free will? If we accepted your theory of this country, then there really is no hope for the black race unless we all take up arms. So why don't we all just give up and stay home collecting welfare checks? Under your theory, that's all we have. If America's sole purpose is holding back the black man, how do you explain our progress so far? White appeasement? You are diminishing all the sacrifices our ancestors made to get us to where we are today by chalking up our great strides in this country to nothing more than white people throwing us some bones. Why is it so hard to believe that although racism does exist, opportunities to improve one's condition do too? And we should use them.

> But that's cool, you can stand in line for 30 minutes at your check cashing place and then hold me up in the post office line getting your seven money orders if you want to. I can't waste my time being mad at you; I got money to make. A reparations check? You want the government to send Negroes who have never been enslaved, never been brutalized, and likely have a Lincoln Navigator outside of their apartments, an MFing check? Get a life. Better yet—get a job.

Just as we plan our lives, **we must also plan our deaths.** Sure, death is uncomfortable and creepy to talk about, but getting your business affairs in order and your estate planned will pay off in spades. I know so many families who are financially decimated simply because a loved one neglected to draw up a will. It is inexcusable not to have one, especially if you have children or siblings and own property.

One of the biggest problems in the African American community is that we rarely pass down wealth to the next generation. As my mother says, "It seems black folks are always starting over." When you do not have a will and no written instructions for how you want your property or belongings distributed, what usually happens is that your family ends up selling everything and splitting the money. The house you lived in all your life and paid every note on is gone. The antiques and art you collected are gone. And sadly, in a couple years,

- ❏ Plan your death. Make a will! Today.

- ❏ Saving is not a luxury. No matter how little you earn, save SOMETHING. This could ultimately protect your family from crisis in the event of unemployment, disability, or other emergency.

that money that everyone divided amongst themselves is pissed up, and there is nothing left to show of your assets but some old photographs in a shoebox that no one can find. And then they start over.

When your assets are distributed as you instruct, someone stays in your home, someone is entrusted to your art, and someone else takes over that piece of rental property. Now your family can start to build on what you have accomplished. In leaving a house for someone specific to live in and raise their family in, you give the next generation a leg-up on accumulating wealth. They can now save the money they would have spent on a house to invest in a business or send their kids to college. The rental property income now assists a new family and your grandkids. It makes their lives easier and affords them more opportunities.

Estate planning is taboo in the black community, and the lack of it results in a lot of cash payouts, the loss of real estate, and everyone starting again from scratch. I actually heard a woman say, "Why should I give everything to my kids? They should have to work for it like I did." What an idiot. Write a will, people. Stop starting over.

Always have a plan for your financial security. The most important concept to the growth of wealth is **save, save, save.** When you face an unexpected health crisis, car repair, or other financial hardship, your closet full of shoes will not help one bit. There is a Chinese proverb that states that the saving man becomes the free man. When you have money in the bank, you don't have to live with a constant anxiety of the unexpected cost. Though improving, the saving rate of most Americans is dreadful. For black Americans the numbers are even worse. When you have nothing saved, there is no room for error in your life; to live in constant fear, waiting for the other shoe to drop, just ain't livin'.

The second most important concept in the accumulation of wealth is **to invest your money in things that appreciate**. Not things that YOU appreciate, but things that appreciate in value. Despite the recent economic downturn, real estate, stocks and bonds, and precious metals are still considered secure long-term investments. These are items that make you money while you're asleep. They grow in value and can be used as collateral to acquire more. If you have the luxury, then you may be interested in other items that appreciate like high art and fine wine, stamps and coins. As you become more financially sophisticated, so can your investments. As I said before, contribute the maximum to your 401(k); it's a painless way to accumulate a healthy nest egg for your retirement.

Another way to invest in yourself is **starting a business**. More and more of us want to be entrepreneurs. Technology has made it easier for people to do so and thrive with relatively low overhead costs. I think it's a great trend, and I'm all about entrepreneurship, but if you choose to use your money to start a business, be certain you do your homework.

The majority of businesses fail because of poor planning. Consult with a professional to ensure a successful business. There are also many universities and government agencies, including the Small Business Administration, that are happy to provide free assistance. Expenses, cash flow, marketing budget, petty cash, advertising, managing employees—these are the fundamentals of running a business that many of us overlook in our excitement to be business owners. I hate seeing all the storefronts and small businesses boarded up in my neighborhood simply because the owners didn't take the time to really do it right. Find someone who knows how to run the business you're interested in and ask them to help you. You may be able to fly by the seat of your pants in everything else, but you never want to run a business that way.

- Realize that debt is the new slavery.
- Whenever you feel the need to show everyone that you have a little money, remember that Bill Gates has a very modest wardrobe and Bob Johnson wears no bling.

Third, **get out of debt** as soon as you can. Neither a borrower nor lender be, as Shakespeare so eloquently stated. Debt is a smothering force. It creates stress and strain on marriages and families. Thomas

Jefferson said, "Our business is to have great credit and use it little." He knew that debt is a hindrance to any kind of personal financial growth. As in slavery, we belong to him whose shackles we wear, and we don't want excessive consumer debt to be our new 21st-century shackles. And unlike our savings accounts, our debts are growing and growing. We rob Peter to pay Paul, but soon Peter, Paul, AND Kevin are going to need to be paid on the same day. And you want to be ready. Just think of going to bed at night knowing you don't owe anyone a damn dime. Now make it happen!

But none of this is easy. Wealth and financial security are rarely achieved by hitting a big number or getting a big record deal. It's all about planning and sacrifice and hard work. This is a universal challenge for us all, regardless of race or socioeconomic status. From life to death, money can assure you a peaceful, secure existence, or it can be a shackle that holds you back from achieving your dreams. Your dreams should be bigger than just DVD players in your headrests. Your dreams should acknowledge all the potential that exists for your life and the lives of your children.

Think wisely! Don't sabotage your success with choices that make no sense. Lotteries, rented bedroom sets, tax evasion, check cashing, blowing untold sums on club-life bullshit—if these are the choices you make with your money, then there is really no one to blame for your financial condition but you. The White Man did not order that bottle of Veuve Clicquot for you at the club.

If you look at money as a means to attaining your wildest dreams and a tool that can sustain you throughout your golden years if used correctly, then you are ahead of the game. Whether you are an entrepreneur or are just trying to make a dollar out of 15 cents, there are many books, nonprofit organizations, and Web sites that can help you achieve your financial goals and tailor a plan for yourself based on your current financial condition. Books by Suze Orman, Michelle Singletary, and Jane Bryant Quinn are great places to start. Of course I can't forget to mention the classic *Think and Grow Rich* by Napoleon Hill. It's a book that focuses on the mentality behind success through visualization techniques. It's like an old school *The Secret*, though, between you and me, the whole visualization thing wears thin after about four pages. "Visualize what you want for your life and you can achieve it!" OK, OK, I got it.

There are also nonprofit organizations like AARP, the Urban League, Credit.org, SCORE, and NACA that are there solely to help you get it together. Many cities have free legal clinics and free tax preparation services that can be vital in helping you understand your economic situation and learning how to improve it. Or, you could always just log off Facebook for a few minutes and search the rest of the Internet for free resources that could possibly help you.

So let's not only challenge each other to dream big, but also to plan big and act big. Although the media makes us think that money and success are easy, that they are things that just fall out of the sky, nothing can be further from the truth. Whatever stage of life you are in, you should always have a plan for success, be it financial or otherwise. And in this global age, it is more important than ever that we all have plans and goals for our lives. Short-term stuff can be taken away from you. Education, achievement, and financial literacy are forever.

Is the financially responsible approach fun all the time? Hell no. Is there sacrifice involved? Absolutely. But when you are kicking back at midlife on a fabulous vacation, you'll be happy you did it. So have a little fun, make the tough decisions, and most of all, when it comes to your money and your future, use some common damn sense. It's never too late to start using your money wisely. And you can take that to the bank.

My Uncle Art had a great saying that I live by: "It's all right to be old and it's all right to be poor—just don't let them hit you at the same time."

8

GROWING PAINS:
WHERE ARE THE LEADERS?

"I don't wear a jersey, I'm 30 plus"—*Jay-Z*

Twenty years ago things were simple. They were orderly. The North had its music; the South had its music. The West Coast had its style of dress; the East Coast had its style, and never the twain shall meet. You could tell where someone was from by the hairstyle. Gold streaks: New York. Rainbow streaks: Baltimore. You listened to one radio station, and your parents listened to another. Those were the days. The days before media conglomerates became a part of our households, gradually homogenizing our culture across geographic and generational lines. Thanks, FCC!

Nowadays, for better or worse, all those distinctions are gone. Because of the pervasiveness of the media, the same images and fashion and culture are transmitted into our homes and into our ears simultaneously across the country all day, every day. This has resulted in everyone generally dressing the same, listening to the same music, and chasing the same glamorous yet elusive lifestyles.

This increasing cultural homogeneity also now applies to generational distinctions, which is where I think we have gotten into trouble.

There once was a time when you didn't listen to the same radio station as your parents. You didn't watch the same shows or even the same channel. But now, we all are watching, listening to, and often wearing the same thing. It's hard to tell where a young person ends and a grown-ass person begins.

> ❏ **Leadership starts by being the example.**
>
> ❏ **We all have a role in transforming our communities.**

If we are all ingesting the same bad influences, the same 24 hours of broadcasted pathos, then who is left to be the keepers of the moral compass in our communities? The media conglomerates have virtually ensured that we all like the same thing. But is that healthy? Should mothers and daughters really be sitting down watching 106 & Park together? Arguing who is cuter, Trey Songz or Flo-Rida? What happens to kids when there is no one to shut off *Flavor of Love* or *For the Love of Ray J* because the parents are watching too? Sometimes I grow concerned that there is no one around to teach kids how to be adults.

We go to the same clubs, listen to the same music, buy the same DVDs. We both do the Stank Leg and the Cupid Shuffle and yearn to pop bottles with models. Where there was once a vast difference between being 20 and 30, now it's almost indistinguishable. The problem is, if we are all acting like we're 21, who will become the next leaders in the community? Who do young people look to as examples of how to behave when the grown-ups are bending over and touching their toes in the club right next to them?

We used to have a built-in default leadership network in our communities. It was called the black church. It was our greatest champion and led some of the most important cultural and civil rights movements in history. We looked to it for guidance, news, social services, fellowship, and some good fried fish on Fridays. When the traditional familial structure wasn't available to someone, or when they perhaps just found themselves alone in a sea of distress, they could always find a helping hand and a good song at the black church.

Even that has changed. Where we once had a benevolent force on every corner that was always there when we needed it, many churches have turned into irrelevant money pits, leeching off the very communities that give it life. At some point during the last two decades, the institution we had come to know and love, our beloved black church that had been so instrumental in the gains of black folks throughout the last century, just seemed to fade into obscurity.

Many theorize that the reduced role of the church in the communities is at the root of many of our current social ills. The black church has become a shell of its former self. It is now known more for its celebrity preachers, expensive cars, and long suit jackets than being at the forefront of social progress. In his 2008 article for CNN on the role of the modern-day black church, John Blake discusses how the focus on social issues has been replaced by "prosperity preaching." He observes that the black churches very rarely "follow Martin Luther King's prophetic model of ministry—one that confronted political and economic institutions of power," and instead now focus on a message that concentrates primarily on the acquisition of wealth.

In the face of cultural crises like black-on-black violence, high-school dropouts, disintegrating family structures, and the HIV/AIDS epidemic in our communities, churches have been largely silent, instead diverting our attention onto the riches we could all attain if we just follow God's word. They seem to be too busy telling everyone that they're about to hit the lottery to provide essential social services for local communities.

Regardless of the chaos in the communities surrounding the church and the shattered lives of its parishioners, it seems the church has adopted the position of a theological Dr. Feelgood. Blake spoke to Edward Wheeler, president of the Christian Theological Seminary in Indianapolis, about this new wave of prosperity preaching. Wheeler replied, "You don't generally build huge churches by making folks uncomfortable on Sunday morning." As long as they can get the congregation shouting and passing the offering plate, then everyone is happy. And that's part of the problem—this fear of telling each other the truth about our condition and the congregation's refusal to hold churches accountable to the very people who support them.

It's particularly hard to swallow when studies have shown that churchgoers with incomes between $10,000 and $40,000 per year were found to donate more to the church than any other group. The study, conducted by the Interdenominational Theological Center in Atlanta, spanned two years and examined more than 200 churches. Those with the least to give often give the most.

How do I take seriously institutions that, in the name of God, build megachurches instead of refinancing bad loans for their congregations? How do you look to the pulpit for leadership in the community when the pastor has a wife and a baby mama in the same pew? An ATM in the lobby? Really? But you can't refinance my home loan?

It's funny how churches have seemed to succumb to all the abuses and excesses of the hip-hop culture they so often deride. The churches have become just as materialistic and flamboyant as the hottest rap stars. With Bentleys, Gucci wallpaper, private planes, and jewelry being the mark of a successful preacher, it's hard to tell 'em from the playas.

Let me give you an example of when I knew something was dreadfully off. It was a Sunday morning like any other. The urban church show was in full swing. Mostly unaccompanied women and gay men trickled into the pews. The church's favorite time-filler, Praise and Worship, went on at full volume. I usually try to get to church AFTER that damn Praise and Worship part; it's annoying, and I never know if I'm supposed to be standing up. Anyway, the service started, and, turns out, it was the First Lady's birthday. So here came offering plate number one and everyone was supposed to give an offering for her birthday. Personally, I don't know why I should give a shit; I don't know her, and she sure as hell didn't get me anything for my birthday. But I let that ride.

So there's more church stuff: some singing, holy ghosting, touching your neighbor, and whatnot. Then out came offering plate number two, something called a love offering. Now, a love offering is something that no one seems able to define. Even those within the church begin to stumble and stutter when asked what, exactly, the purpose of a love offering is. The best explanation I've heard is that it's an offering to show appreciation to the pastor and his wife. Not Jesus, but the pastor and his wife. Chile, appreciate these.

OK, more wafer eating, grape juice drinking (coming off a night of drinking, it's so yummy!), more neighbor touching, singing, and some announcements. Say it ain't so, here came offering plate number three. Now this is the "regular" offering. The offering that you were used to, the offering that you expected. The one that sent your hard-earned money (that you had given out of guilt because you just couldn't bear to pass that plate by without putting anything in it) into some locked office down some back steps you never descend.

Now here came the big mama, the RUFKM moment. This church, going into hour two, announced there would be another offering. Offering number four would be an offering to help the church bring down its debt. Apparently they knew that we all got wise to that fake-ass building fund, and now they're talking about debt reduction. The pastor had the unmitigated gall and colossal nerve to ask this church, whose members are generally middle- and lower-income urbanites, to give $1,000 to help reduce the church's debt burden.

This is the same church that did an altar call a little while back and asked all those who had a home that was in danger of foreclosure to come to the front. Hundreds of worshippers went to the front of the church that morning. You know what he did for them? Prayed.

This is the same church that sits in the middle of an urban center whose unemployment rate tops 15 percent. What in the hell would Jesus do if he knew that his chosen ones were asking their flocks for $1,000 in the midst of a recession? What would Jesus do if he knew his chosen ones were asking those who may be homeless in 30 days to help service the church's debt? What would Jesus do if he knew they were passing around four offering plates in communities they knew had few means to support their own families?

What happened to churches that led us and reacted to the needs of the communities instead of using us as an ATM? Instead of asking for $1,000 to service your church's debt, shouldn't you be asking for money to start a fund to help keep people in their homes? The offering for the First Lady's birthday probably could have gotten 20 families current on their mortgages. Even my pagan ass would contribute to that. That cause is something I would happily put money into the plate for.

I'm just appalled by the insensitivity and lack of empathy for their "flocks." Aren't the churches supposed to take care of us, not the other way around? It isn't our fault you went and built some megachurch you could barely afford. We were all just fine in the old building.

Is there any wonder that the churches have become obsolete in the movement for social causes? We are facing the biggest financial crisis in a generation, and we need more than some secondhand clothes and new backpacks. Why can't you use the offerings that we make without fail, every Sunday, to help us in our time of need? It reminds me of insurance companies; you pay and pay and pay into your policy, and then when you really need something, they don't want to give you anything.

Churches should be about service, not self-serving. We must get away from the church version of *American Idol,* where every church wants star status. Where every pastor longs for gators, a long-ass suit jacket, and a TV show. Somewhere along the way we forgot about the real mission of the church, which is service to humanity. The relationship shouldn't be one-way. It should be symbiotic: the church supports the community, and the community supports the church. However, too many churches take, take, take and then drive back to their McMansions in the suburbs, leaving the flock to fend for itself.

Have they become so disconnected from the communities they "serve" that they would really believe that asking for four offerings in a service is acceptable? Do they really think that asking a lower-income congregation to donate $1,000 to service the church's debt is Christlike? Have they become so out of touch and so used to free money that they've forgotten that it's a GOD-damned recession? I sure hope not. I want you to touch your neighbor and say, "Shame on you."

Now I'm not condemning all churches—there are churches out there that are filling necessary voids in social services and providing support to needy families who are down on their luck. But to the rest of the churches who are just acting as leeches on a community that is already low on lifeblood, I hope they think about their true calling. I hope their congregations begin to hold them accountable for their lack of service to the very communities that support them.

And serving is not just offering Sunday school or watching people's kids while they are in church. How are you gonna offer a potluck dinner for $12 a plate? And just where the hell is all the bingo money going? Maybe we don't need another bus trip to a casino. Give us something we really need, like food, clothing, shelter, or a mortgage payment. You have the opportunity to be a lifeline for so many, and really, isn't that what Jesus would do?

Meanwhile, even though the new crop of megachurches has enormous potential for galvanizing large populations of African Americans in the name of important social issues, these churches rarely venture into the arenas of politics, social justice, or cultural issues.

The black church is dealing with a loss of faith. We have lost faith in them and their leadership in our communities. The institutions that were the backbone of the civil rights movement have pretty much turned into irrelevant, behind-the-times dinosaurs. We have all-women social clubs bowing at the feet of a male demigod who takes their tithes and buys diamond earrings for himself and his wife. And his girlfriend. (I know, I'm going to hell.)

So as we lose our leaders in the communities and lose our leaders in the church, we are facing a huge leadership void that each and every one of us must make every attempt to fill. We don't have the luxury of sticking our heads in the sand and hoping someone else will step up and do our jobs for us.

Many adults are choosing to exist in the purgatory between being grown and being a child. Like the *Twilight* vampires (or the Anne Rice vampires for the old heads), never aging but eternally 18 years old. And unfortunately, this eternal youth is permeating other aspects of our lives and causing major problems.

Like 18-year-olds, we are irresponsible with our finances, with our choice of mates, and with our decisions regarding sex, children, and morality. It's like we want our whole lives to be that party at the club we see on all the videos, every day, all day. Like children, we want what we want and want it now. We live in a self-centered world that we feel should revolve around us. We act impulsively, guided by our ids, and rarely consider the consequences of our actions. We're big, stretch-mark-having, drowning-in-debt teenagers.

And like teenagers who have gotten into trouble, we make excuses for what has gone wrong in our lives and place the blame on others. My bills aren't paid because they must have lost my money order. I'm unemployed because that company doesn't like black people. I have three kids by three different people because niggas ain't shit. At what point will we grow up?

Single parents struggling to make ends meet still get to the club or have the latest ringtone or that dress Beyoncé had on in that video. We've become high school grownups. Women out-drinking their daughters at the club are MIA at parent-teacher conferences.

Sure, I'll be the first one to agree that 30 is the new 20, but being young at heart has its limitations. Just because you feel 20 doesn't mean you should act like it.

What happened to the grown-ups being the role models for appropriate behavior and dress? How do we teach our young women that there is more to them than their physical appearance and their sexuality when their mamas are going out in painted-on jeans, no bra, and stilettos? How do we teach our young men how to dress appropriately when their dads have 12 pairs of Timberland boots and not one suit?

We can't all be Lil Wayne and Lil' Kim our whole lives. At some point we have to be big people. I happen to believe there is age-appropriate behavior and dress. At 40, do you really need your pants hanging down past your drawers? I know you think it looks cool. I know you think it makes you looks young, but it looks ridiculous. If you were born in the '60s, you should no longer be wearing cornrows. That's real talk. We can't blame our children for being under the spell of the negative images fed to them by the media when we are eating it up as well. Parents are busy trying to give their four-year-old the Chris Brown look (yes, even now) with a mohawk and an earring, but no one is buying him a book.

> ❑ Face it; you aren't 20 anymore. Stop acting like it. There is a difference between being young at heart and being the old guy at the club.
>
> ❑ We have a responsibility to mentor, educate, and guide the next generation, not be their friends and drinking buddies.

We must put the health of our communities and our children ahead of our petty needs and dysfunctional desire to be Rihanna (yes, even now). I know that's your favorite song, but is it really appropriate for a seven-year-old in the car? I know you may want to see that R-rated movie, but do you really drag your eight-year-old there because you can't find a sitter? African American children are already exposed to so many negative images that it is important we not reinforce them at home. We must lead by example in word and deed. We must be their leaders.

Every other day I receive an Internet video of some little girl dancing suggestively as adults cheer her on. A REAL grown-up would sit that little girl down and tell her that they had better not catch her dancing like that again. But this new breed of fake grown-ups runs to get the video camera. And then posts it on the Internet! We're encouraging our little girls to hump floors and pop their coochies? If the adults in the neighborhood don't lead the kids in the right direction and give them guidance and education on proper behavior and how to conduct themselves, who will? Where is the new generation of leaders?

When I hear of parents getting into fights with teachers and other students, or I see parents on the bus with their children cussing at them, it makes me wonder what happened to the breed of human called the "adult." Are we all so hypnotized by the spell of hip-hop and the lure of street life that we've forgotten it's our responsibility to lead the next generation? How can we lead them when we are trying to party with them instead? Are you really a standard-bearer for the community when you are 38 and busy chatting up 18-year-olds on MySpace? How can these men and women shape the agenda for the black community when their worlds revolve around being ballers and vixens?

Putting on a throwback jersey, braiding up your hair, letting your pants sag low, and having a pair of Jordans for each day of the week doesn't give you license to act like a 16 year old. As much as you may wish you were 16, it's time to give it up and handle your business. We need adults in the community. We have enough wannabe young thugs. We have enough hoochie mamas and baby mamas. We are lacking sophisticated, real-life grown-ups. Louis Farrakhan said, "Whenever we stop growing, we start deteriorating."

Being an adult is a state of mind—the state of mind of being responsible for one's decisions, mistakes, and quality of life. Adults are accountable for their choices and take responsibility for them. They know it is
no one's responsibility but their own to support them or clean up their
messes.

It is up to the adults to lead. We have to show our young people how
to live, how to succeed. How do young people form a work ethic? Where
do they learn the value of education? Where do they learn what a healthy
romantic relationship is? How will they learn to be good parents? When
you are on *Maury* giving paternity tests to six guys, are you really leading? Parents and other adults in the community should be the leaders
in teaching kids morals and enforcing standards and expectations, but
instead we're too busy proving how youthful we are and that we can still
hang with the young folks at the club.

How can the adults teach what they don't practice? Children should
learn early about the responsibilities of working and making a living for
oneself. But how do you teach your kids the value of hard work when
your main occupation is being a fake grown-up and sitting home waiting on checks?

Are you really an adult when you are using child support or your
kid's social security as your sole source of income? If that money was
intended to support YOU, it would be called alimony/spousal support.
You shouldn't be paying rent and utilities and making up for the fact
that you aren't *working* with a child support or social security check.
Child support and social security are there to supplement your income,
take care of any special needs of the child, and replicate the monetary
benefits of a two-income household. It's for your child, not you. It's to
help support the child; it's not a revenue stream. Money for your kids is
money for your kids. It's not the lottery. Jeez Louise.

Are you really an adult when you support yourself with a fake-ass disability check? Please don't get me started on all the fake-ass disability
(FAD) going on out here. Of course, I'm not talking about the really

disabled people. I'm talking about the fake-ass, I-got-into-a-car-accident-in-1987 people on the government's bank roll. I have met sooooo many people on FAD recently. I mean, should you really be on disability if you are able to have sex, have children, and get into fights in front of your building? If you can get up and take care of three kids, two of which you've had since you were "disabled," then you can take your ass to work. I met this dude on disability that, by the looks of him, could have been a personal trainer at Gold's Gym. But he had "back pain" that prevented him from working (although he played flag football on the weekends and made two babies).

Are you really an adult when your career consists of waiting on a settlement to come through? Oh, the elusive settlement check. Everyone raise their hand if they know someone who is waiting for a settlement check. These folks have had some shady-ass personal injury or been in a suspicious car accident and then called one of those lawyers on TV. That bruise could be worth tens of thousands! So 35 chiropractor visits and a 40 percent contingency fee later, they are waiting for that check that will make all their dreams come true. They don't have to work because they are waiting on their settlements. They borrow money from you with the promise of paying it back when they get their checks. Does the settlement ever come?

So many of us claiming to be adults are really only interested in getting a check for nothing. I guess it's good non-work if you can get it. But after a while, don't you start to feel like a loser? Whereas in our parents' generation no one wanted the stigma of being on the government rolls, folks today are just looking for a roll to be on. Because of "adults" like this, there is a whole generation of kids who have never seen a mom or dad leave the house in the morning and come home in the evening with a paycheck for the work they did. So is it really a surprise when our kids slowly but surely become adults who want something for nothing? Who refuse to be accountable for their mistakes and have no clue as to the concept of consequences?

We must prepare our kids for the real world. We must show them what it means to be adults or we'll end up with a world of perpetual teenagers who want everything to be easy, who forever avoid taking responsibility for their own lives. Marian Wright Edelman, former head of the Children's Defense Fund, says of the importance of parents and leadership, "If you are a parent, recognize that it is the most important calling and rewarding challenge you have. What you do every day, what you say, and how you act will do more to shape the future of America than any other factor." She implores the nation's parents to become part of our future by becoming positively engaged with our children. There is no more important task.

JAM THE NEGRO

Adults not acting like adults? What the hell are you talking about now? I don't know where you come from, but I know I'm a grown-ass woman. What difference does it make what I wear and what I listen to on the radio? As long as I'm taking care of my business, who cares? And if I have the body to pull off some Daisy Dukes at 35, then I should be applauded, not put through the ringer by you. You are probably just mad that you can't wear that two-piece at the beach anymore. Well, tough luck. Serves you right, the way you talk about people. There are plenty of examples in the community for kids to look up to. All these hard-working moms out here busting their asses to raise their kids alone, and you want to call them bad examples? Sorry if everyone is not Martha Stewart or leading some perfect life. This is reality, and truth be told, most parents are just doing the best they can. And why are you worried about how someone makes a living? Whether it's a job or a check, what's the difference as long as food gets on the table? You're saying if you got injured in an accident, you're not going to sue and try to get paid? I thought so. You're a lawyer, so you probably know all the tricks. I think you are being overdramatic and overreacting as usual. You are creating problems where there are none. It doesn't matter what adults wear, how they talk, or how they make a living. At the end of the day, if they are handling their business, it's all good with me.

JAM THE AMERICAN

Jesus, take the wheel. If you can't see how an adult's behavior can negatively impact the lives of children, then you are nucking futs. If you don't see the need for positive examples in urban communities, then I don't know what to tell you. How can we teach the next generation anything when we are showing our asses at the same time? Children imitate what they see. So sue me if I don't think your thong is something a five-year-old needs to be exposed to. Sorry if I think that having an actual job is a good example to set for children. There needs to be some delineation between the grown-ups and the kids. And that just becomes more difficult when we're all at the same party. There are so few positive role models in the inner city that it is imperative we encourage our adults to take the extra steps to mentor and guide our young people. Even if you don't do it formally, it is a great service to the neighborhood just to act with dignity and respect. You'd be amazed how far that goes. We want our kids to know what it means to work hard, be rewarded, and be respected when they walk into a room. It is our job to show them what that means, what that looks like. So you can sit around in your Daisy Dukes, surfing MySpace, downloading ringtones while watching BET, and waiting for the mailman to arrive with your check if you want to—just don't be surprised when you look up in 10 years and your kids are fat losers on the sofa waiting for checks of their own.

No conversation about leadership in the black community is complete without talking about our 44th president of the United States, Barack Obama. Barack Obama, a hero of mine, has redefined leadership in the country. He is a shining example of what can be accomplished with commitment and determination. He is educated, works hard, and takes being a husband and father seriously. His election to office was the single most important historical moment I've experienced in my lifetime. I was able to attend his inauguration and forgot all about the cold and my aching feet when I saw that brother walking down the hall on his way to the Capitol steps. It beat out the previous winner, the Million Man March, by a mile.

His election has changed me, like it has changed most Americans, in a fundamental way. The paradigm has suddenly shifted. The concept of limitations on one's potential in life changed in a single day. It is so awe inspiring to know that an entire generation of children won't look at Barack Obama as the first *black* president; he'll just be the president to them. They will have no preconceived notions on who can and cannot be president of these United States. That concept is invaluable. All that being said, I have an Obama-related issue.

It all started with the coverage of the 2008 presidential election. You saw countless interviews with members of the African American community standing in lines across the country, speaking about how proud they were to have a chance to vote for the first black president. Don't get me wrong; even I teared up as I cast my ballot for Obama, but as I watched the interviews with various voters throughout the day, something started to bother me. I began to notice how many times I heard things like "I haven't voted in 15 years, but I'm inspired to vote for Obama." Or a 40-year-old man saying something like, "I've never voted before, but I'm here to vote for Obama." There were so many black folks saying that they never thought it was important to vote until Obama's candidacy, so many black folks saying Obama made them believe in the political process again.

Now as inspirational as Obama's candidacy is, I still couldn't help but bristle a bit at the number of folks who never attached any importance to voting until Obama came along. Why did it take a black presidential candidate to make black people interested in presidential politics? A community whose parents and grandparents died for the right to vote somehow felt content staying home until a black man ran for president. RUFKM?

After the 2008 vote, the nation declared a new president and suddenly there were all these interviews talking about how there's a new image of the black male. That men are suddenly going to start pulling their pants up and gaining some pride in their images because of Obama. Educated is now the new cool, and success will no longer be measured in bling and bitches. I heard an interview on Michel Martin's *Tell Me More* on NPR in which she spoke to moms who were so happy that their sons now had a role model other than rappers and athletes. There was a new quest for excellence in the black community, and Obama was leading the parade.

We heard speculation about how this may be a new age in the black family. The black family may make a comeback because of the Obamas.

We now had a real life *Cosby Show* to look to for examples of a successful nuclear family. It's a brand new day in the black community!

Is it me, or is this a little scary? Our community wasn't inspired by our children getting gunned down in the streets. Our community didn't get inspired by a 50 percent drop-out rate. Our community wasn't inspired to vote when they heard that only 25 percent of registered black voters in Florida voted in the crucial 2000 election, when we could have single-handedly changed the results of the election and, consequently, the course of history. Our community wasn't inspired by our wedlock rate and the lack of black marriage. Our community wasn't inspired by the cultural pathos that runs rampant in our streets everyday. We weren't inspired by the sorry condition of our inner cities and the lack of morality bred in our children.

> ❑ **We all have the ability to be leaders, whether it's in our homes, communities, or schools.**

We weren't inspired by the fact that most black children grow up without a father in the home. We weren't inspired by the million black men in prison. We weren't inspired by the fact that so many black children place no value in education, choosing instead to seek out the models of success as taught to them by hip-hop. We weren't inspired by an underlying adversarial relationship between our men and women. But a black president? Shiiiit, it must be time for change!

Let me get this straight: a black man runs for president and wins, and all of a sudden we're inspired and want to get our shit together? Doesn't that scare you just a little bit? It lends credence to the notion that without a magical Negro leader, black folks are lost. And sure, I'm a little torn. I'm conflicted about even saying this out loud, but something just sticks in my proverbial craw about Obama inspiring us to do things that witnessing children dying on the streets right before our eyes couldn't do. Are we that desperate for a savior? We don't give two squirts of duck crap about doing better until Obama wins? Huh?

Our communities have been floundering for years—why does it take one man to convince us we have the ability to act on our own behalf for positive change in our own communities? Why does Obama suddenly make us care? Why do we always seem to depend on someone else to give us value? Do we not think we're important enough? Is it the long-rumored, America-inspired self-hatred where we inherently feel that we are not worthy without the validation of others? Obama has now given us value so we can feel good again? We can suddenly be inspired again to do better in our lives? We now have permission?

I don't know. I mean, anything that achieves forward progress and makes folks want to do better is all right with me. But the notion that it has to be attached to a person or a movement and isn't an eternal fire in our bellies bothers me. For centuries we have relied on a collective quest to overcome. A collective notion of success and equality. We were our brothers' keepers, and we kept our eyes on the prize. But now we seem insecure in our journey toward self-actualization. Our communities are so misdirected and disjointed and lacking structure that we are totally lost without someone ramming a message or slogan or T-shirt motto down our throats.

We seem to thirst for leadership. We want so desperately for someone to validate what we know already: that we are smart, powerful people with the ability to achieve anything; that we are survivors and the strongest of the strong, capable of succeeding in spite of any challenge. But without someone telling us and showing us, we just don't quite believe it. We want to believe it, and in our quiet moments, or as we shout in church, we tell ourselves that we are great and that God is good. Then we leave and go back to our every-man-for-himself lives, deftly navigating the duality DuBois spoke of but never really succeeding at either. Never knowing what to believe or what to do. Until someone shows us.

John Hope Franklin, one of our nation's most respected scholars and historians, in an interview with Gwen Ifill for *The NewsHour*, made a great point about Dr. Martin Luther King Jr. that is eerily relevant to

President Barack Obama. He acknowledged that, although our community needs leadership, he felt that there was an "unfortunate cult of personality related to Dr. King." He went on to say, "When you place all of your stock on a particular person or even a group of people, then I think you are failing to see what the ordinary person's role is in the transformation of society." He cautioned, "We must not place so much emphasis on a leader and think about the responsibility of all of us."

I think of Dr. Franklin's words when I see that so many of us had no interest at all in the political process or the state of our communities until Barack Obama came along. Don't get me wrong, I'm glad he's my president, I'm glad he inspired people, and I think he's the cat's pajamas, BUT he won't be the president forever, and we can't let who is in the White House dictate the interest we have in saving our communities.

In the meantime, even if it is solely Obama-inspired, I hope we do start to rethink our leadership roles in our communities. We need leaders all day, every day in the home, at school, on the streets, in churches, at work, on the bus, and anywhere else where we can make a difference to young people. We need to show them how it's done.

We need *you*. Nelson Mandela said that "to be free is not merely to cast off one's chains, but to live in a way that respects and enhances the freedom of others." We need your input, your examples, your wisdom. We need adults to make their presence known in the community. We need you to be a beacon in the night for our young people. Not only should you live your life as an example to others, you should also take an active role in your community. We need more mentors, more volunteers, more tutors, more men and women to assist the elderly, more doctors, more lawyers, more social workers, more role models. We need more leaders. We have enough bitches and thugs.

9

THE TALENTED TENTH HAS LET US DOWN

"Service is the rent you pay for room on this earth."
—*Shirley Chisholm*

Most people use the term Talented Tenth (TT) to describe some supposed elite class of black folks, a class that is educated, conscious, and the community's best hope for advancement and progress. Unfortunately, many of us who use the term are not aware of its full history and the mandate that goes along with being a part of this TT community.

The Talented Tenth was first written about by black educator and author W. E. B. DuBois in 1903 as a part of a collection of articles by African Americans called *The Negro Problem*. "The Talented Tenth" was the second chapter of the collection. It emphasized the necessity for higher education to develop the leadership capacity among the most able 10 percent of black Americans.

These days the black bourgeoisie love to throw this term around (generally to describe themselves to other people like them). However, what most people don't seem to realize, or maybe they just choose to ignore, is that there is another dimension to the Talented Tenth. See, the Talented Tenth wasn't meant to be some elite social club. The Talented Tenth isn't the Links or the Moles or Jack and Jill or the Boule or all those other snobby black social clubs. (A quick aside: I was at some function thrown by the Moles and I heard one of the members call another woman "a waste of light skin." I figured a paper bag test—which I would undoubtedly fail—was next. I pretty much ran out of there screaming with my arms flailing overhead.) What many of these self-described Talented Tenthers don't seem to realize is that DuBois believed the Talented Tenth had a specific purpose and, more importantly, a mission. DuBois charged this elite group with the task of being "leaders of thought" and "missionaries of culture." Imagine that—the privileged class actually having to do something.

And it's the second half of the Talented Tenth philosophy that has gotten lost in the proverbial sauce over the last century. We are all fine with being upper-crust, but being thought of as leaders and cultural missionaries? Who has the time for that crap?

So therein lies the problem: the black folks who have been standing on the shoulders of giants have been wearing spiked shoes. We are more than happy to take advantage of all the opportunities our ancestors fought for. We are more than happy to go to all the fancy schools our grandparents fought to go to, live in the fancy neighborhoods our grandparents fought to get into, take all the jobs our grandparents fought for us to have. Oh sure, we love to reap the benefits, but the sowing part, not so much.

It seems the concept of charity and service has been lost in a sea of BMWs, McMansions, flat screen TVs, Ivy League schools, iPods, liposuction, and Manolo Blahniks. Sure, you may have participated in some bone marrow drive your freshman year, or you went and served

Thanksgiving dinner to the homeless once, or maybe you dropped off all your now-too-tight clothes at the Salvation Army. And then you have the nerve to list that on your resume as community service? It's a damn shame. Shirley Chisholm said, "Service is the rent you pay for room on this Earth." I guess my generation didn't bother to read the lease.

Concepts like "Am I my brother's keeper?" and "Love thy neighbor" are becoming obsolete. They weren't kidding around when they called us the "me generation." It's officially every person for him- or herself, a philosophical framework that is antithetical to our roots and our history. It was the communal spirit that played such a large part in our extraordinary progress over the last century.

I look around at my friends; some have fancy-shmancy degrees, fancy-shmancy cars, and fancy-shmancy houses. Others don't have fancy-shmancy shit. The one thing they all have in common is that not one of them does community service. I don't seem to have those friends who can't make happy hour because they are out reading to the blind or teaching math or coaching soccer. I don't know anyone who volunteers or tutors or builds those Jimmy Carter houses. Everyone's evening schedule is generally wide open. They can make it to the club before 7:00 P.M. to catch the open bar, but volunteering their time to help those less fortunate, not so much. Why is that?

It's an odd phenomenon, especially in light of the fact that most of my contemporaries were bleeding-heart, fight-the-power liberals who entered college wanting the change the world and help the people. But somewhere between freshman year and the MBA, everyone seemed to say, "To hell with that." I don't know what happened to disenchant us from public service, community activism, and charity.

Sure, everyone signs up to tutor inner-city kids freshman year. We all do the breast cancer walk, the AIDS bike ride. But soon afterward (generally spring semester), we move on to bigger and better things, like pledging sororities, playing spades, interning, playing drinking games, or having sex.

The abandonment of community service and charity crosses all socioeconomic lines. Make no mistake: it's not just a bunch of privileged kids. Even those who came from disadvantaged upbringings said "Fuck it." We ALL forgot. OK, maybe *forgot* is too harsh. We were just so busy looking forward that we never thought to look back.

Many of us '80s babies came from parents with pasts full of struggle. Our parents fought twice as hard to get the opportunities that were readily available to us, their children. They reveled in the fact that their kids wouldn't have to fight the same battles and struggle so hard. A new world was open to their children, and they pushed us to grab as much of it as we could. Unfortunately, too often, the concept of charity got trampled in the race to the top.

It was the '80s: the middle class was rapidly growing. For many families, struggling became a thing of past. People just wanted to wear Jheri curls, listen to Kool and the Gang, and *Celebrate good times, come on*. Forget the Evans family and the Sanfords; we wanted to be the Jeffersons and the Cosbys. And in our haste to be the best and the brightest and have the biggest and the shiniest—our less fortunate brothers and sisters were forgotten.

> ❏ **Make service to others a priority in your life.**

The Black Is Beautiful '70s were over, and we were in the Green Is Beautiful '80s. Community became less important. Many African Americans left the inner city in search of wall-to-wall carpeting, a front yard, and central air conditioning. The inner city became a victim of brain drain and wallet drain. The middle class took its hopes and dreams and its tax revenue and moved the hell out. Some wanted better schools, some wanted better services, and others just wanted to get closer to Whitey because word had it that his ice was colder.

Sure, my generation certainly wasn't delusional about the color line in this country. Our parents, while stressing the opportunities we had for excelling, definitely kept us grounded in terms of the reality of racism. But the lesson was less about the limitations of racism and more about how to work it. For example, my parents always told me that I had to be smarter, work harder, and be more focused than my white counterparts. They taught me how to navigate racism, how to prepare for it, and how to fight it. But racism was never considered a reason for not achieving something. I may have to work a little harder than Muffy and Billy, but success was absolutely possible. And that's how I lived.

So although racism was still a fact of life, there was also a sense that you could make it if you tried. (Wasn't that a song?) Finally, it seemed that we had some control of our destiny. We were no longer relegated to certain schools or jobs or neighborhoods. And in this generational passing of the torch, many of us who took the baton never stopped to think about those who weren't even in the race.

Well, here we are with a black president, and the Talented Tenthers are now a bunch of grown-ass men and women, some doing better than others. We've taken a lot of different roads, but very few have taken the road that includes a U-turn back to the communities from whence we came. What's worse, we feel no shame about it. In fact, it rarely even crosses our minds. I cannot recall a single time when my friends and I were at a swanky bar drinking too-expensive drinks lamenting how we should be doing more community service.

When it comes to giving back to the community, I have found that there are generally two kinds of Talented Tenthers.

Type 1 includes those who know that, theoretically, giving back to the community would be great, but they really don't have any interest (they generally blame it on being too busy). The United States Bureau of Labor Statistics says that volunteerism in general has declined since 2005. Now perhaps President Obama, with his service-oriented agenda, can change that, but the battle is definitely uphill.

Type 2 Talented Tenthers, in a rush of idealism/guilt, have participated in community service, and once thrown into the belly of the beast
said, "Oh hell no."

Strangely enough, I fall into the Type 2 category, and, frankly, we
have the best stories. Leaving law school, I turned down six figures in
order to make the same salary I could have made out of high school so
I could defend the poor and downtrodden and provide legal representation to low-income residents in my city. I thought it would be noble
work. I thought I would be making a difference and changing lives and
all those other things first-year law students tell themselves they want
to do before the big firms come recruiting. And then I actually did it.

When your goal is to help people and change lives, you tend to buy
into this mythology that the people who you will be devoting your life
to actually need your help and that you will be doing them a service by
assisting them. You sit down in your small office surrounded by other
eager do-gooders in bad clothes, all of you ready to make the proverbial
difference. A year later, you look up and realize that it was all bullshit.

OK, maybe not all of it, but enough to make you doubt how much
you're actually helping. Although I lived in an urban environment my
entire life, I had never understood the depths of our problems as a community until I worked for a nonprofit legal services organization.

Unfortunately, I also learned what a huge portion of our current
social ills had nothing to do with the government or public policy. Only
after getting involved on an intimate level with those who were struggling did I realize just how big a role we play in our own failings.

I would sit in my office day after day and listen to person after person make excuse after excuse as to why everything wrong in their lives
was everyone else's fault but theirs. I would meet with people who
would spend an entire day on three buses going to five different government agencies to fill out forms and submit documents for benefits,
but somehow could never find the time to look for a job. Now, I know
this sounds awful, like some right-wing racist conservative spewing

stereotypes about black people, but I lived it. I cannot deny what I saw every day.

Trust me, I wanted to believe that these were victims of the cold, cruel, racist, classist world who really needed help. But what they wanted was not help. It was a handout. I felt like an enabler. Like someone who continues to give liquor to an alcoholic. Yes, the alcoholic feels better and is happy for the moment, but you aren't helping the person improve his or her life.

About 30 percent of my clients truly were victims whom I was happy to help, and I was grateful for every success. They were wonderful, hard-working people trying to do the right thing, and they just needed a little help on their journey. That's what I went to law school for—to help those folks. They were people who had had their rights violated, been swindled, or just made an honest mistake.

However, the other 70 percent of my clients needed to get up, get out, and get something. These folks had learned the system well and had used their low-income status to get everyone else to solve their problems. Their lives were devoted to getting as much out of the system as possible. They were users, and they were using me to maintain their trifling lifestyles.

Some would bitch to me about how they needed a bigger apartment from public housing because they had had another kid. Last I checked, I have to consider my living conditions and my financial state before making the decision to have a child. Why shouldn't you? If you live in a two-bedroom apartment, then maybe having another child in addition to the two you have now isn't your best move. Why should everyone else have to face the consequences of their actions but you? Yet I'm devoting my life and getting paid peanuts to facilitate your lack of responsibility? And you got an attitude? AND you don't show up for your appointments?

I remember a client who wanted me to help her get out of paying rent because of alleged housing code violations (which, by the way, is the oldest trick in the book). So I went to visit her, and trust me when I tell you that her house was beautiful. It was nicer than most of the homes of people I know who have jobs. So here she is, paying about $50 a month on Section 8 and complaining that she shouldn't pay because the paint is flaking around the back door.

But that wasn't the worst of it. When I visited her, she had three grown men in the basement playing video games at two o'clock in the afternoon. Are you kidding me? So let me get this straight: there are four able-bodied adults in the home, and no one could come up with $50 a month to live in this wonderful house? Instead, you want to get me to fight your landlord and defend your decision not to pay rent? Most people have worked all their lives to live in a home like that. You better get one of those shiftless Negroes in the basement to paint that shit and get out of my face.

I know this sounds mean and callous, but dealing with a constant parade of adult-children who think the world owes them a solution to their problems tends to make you a little bitter. However, I say all this to show that I am living proof that even the most well intentioned can find community service frustrating when people take advantage of the services you perform. When those you are trying to help are unappreciative and feel entitled to your services, the work tends to get on your nerves. You begin to resent the very people you are charged to help. You doubt if you are helping at all.

Am I helping that woman by working for her to stay in a home rent-free when she has no right to? Why shouldn't she be held responsible for her financial commitments like the rest of the world? How is allowing her to stiff her landlady helping anyone? The landlady was black, too. I just couldn't do it.

This story is more common than you might think. I heard similar sentiments every day from fellow African American lawyers. One woman said that after working there for three months, she wanted to become a Republican. So many people who try to reach back and help the less fortunate end up getting bit in the ass as a result.

Although I initially pursued public service as a career, most Type 2 Talented Tenthers give back by simply volunteering at schools, doing after-school or summer tutoring, or assisting at Boys and Girls Clubs or recreation centers. Oh, the tales they tell. Here are young men and women who have decided to go back and give back, and they end up running out of those schools and recreation centers faster than Usain Bolt.

It's hard to expect people to volunteer when classrooms are like a Fallujah battlefield. By the time you get the kid to sit down and be quiet and stop calling you the b-word because that's not nice, it's time to go home. Our neighborhoods, schools, and children are often so out of control that it makes reaching back a tough proposition. It's hard to be effective when you're worrying about your own safety, belligerent parents, or battling apathetic teachers.

 JAM THE NEGRO

You never cease to amaze me. You are the main one telling everyone they have to do better and you aren't doing shit. "Talented Tenth," my eye. You people don't know anything except how to look down your noses at other people who may not have the same fancy college degree as you do. All of us didn't have a mommy and daddy who gave us whatever we wanted. You probably never experienced a hard day's work in your life. And you have the unmitigated gall to sit up here and try to justify your lack of service? It's a damn shame. You are selfish and only focused on one thing: doing you. Just admit it. Don't try to act like the reason you aren't helping is because people are too trifling and kids are too bad. Just acknowledge that you are self-centered, spoiled, and tend to run from anything that presents too much of a challenge. Who said everything was supposed to be easy and convenient for you? Your life is so sheltered and so cushy that you can't be bothered helping others if it takes you out of your comfort zone or your air-conditioned car. You are really sad.

Then you have the nerve to talk about your own clients. People you were entrusted to help. Isn't that against the law to put their business in the streets like that? How can you judge those people? You don't know what was going on in their lives. There may have been plenty of things you didn't know about. For you to characterize those utilizing public benefits as a bunch of lazy scam artists is absurd. I'm sure all those people would go off government benefits if given the opportunity. You think they want to be on public assistance? Of course not. They are using it to transition to a point in their lives when they can be self-sufficient.

All people are not like you or come from backgrounds like yours. Some people have no one to tell them what is the right thing to do, so they have to wander through life trying to figure it out. As for your snooty friends who have had bad experiences in schools, what did they think they were going there to do? This isn't Sesame Street, where everyone is on his or her best behavior all day, every day. These are children, and kids will be kids. But that's right, you and your ilk are waiting later and later to have kids so you can focus on careers, so you probably don't even understand children at all. That's fine, we don't need you and your impatient, elitist friends working with our kids anyway. You will probably just be condescending and insulting. Clearly you have never heard the saying "To whom much is given, much is required." You say you're too busy and then want to point fingers and ask, Why aren't THEY doing better? Maybe because YOU and your pals haven't gone back to help. We can finally agree on one thing: the so-called Talented Tenth have let us down.

JAM THE AMERICAN

I think it's terrible that more people don't volunteer and give back. Would I like to see more people reaching out to help those less fortunate? Of course. But the next question is, would I like to see a lot of those people I'm supposed to be helping get off their asses and help themselves? Of course. It's not so black and white as uppity Negroes refusing to help. Frankly, when I want to tutor or help a child learn to read, that's what I want to do. I don't want to raise your kids, discipline your kids, or fight with your kids. When I want to help provide a service in the community, I want to help provide that service. I don't want to be taken advantage of and abused by a bunch of slackers who are absolutely capable of doing it themselves. Please know that lots of people want to help, but those we are trying to help just don't make it very easy. Sure, it's a cop-out and we should plow forward and do our best regardless of the circumstances, but, damn, what happened to gratitude or appreciation? Don't act like you're doing me any favors by "allowing" me to help you. It's not cool that my radio gets jacked while I'm inside the recreation center trying to teach your kids. I know, those who are needy shouldn't all suffer because of a few bad experiences, but, damn, you get tired of trying to do the right thing and feeling like you're getting shat upon.

I admit I am guilty of not doing enough. Everyone I know is guilty of not doing enough. Mea culpa. But I bust my ass every day. I work my tail off and no one is going to make me feel guilty because I'm not trudging around helping people who don't even want to help themselves. Why are black people the only Americans who are made to feel guilty if we aren't immersing ourselves in the business of helping other black people? Maybe sometimes you just want to be a regular American and enjoy your life and kick back and watch the grass grow. Why does my skin color obligate me to a life of volunteerism? I work hard and play hard, and if feeding the homeless on Christmas is the extent of my charitable contribution to the world, then so be it. No one else is made to feel guilty. You think Koreans are worried about volunteering? No, they're working, trying to make that money. No one challenges that. Sure, I could do more, but how much I do is my business. If I want to stop off after work and have a $12 cocktail, then I should be able to do that without a bunch of self-righteous tree-huggers in their synthetic fabrics looking askance at me. I mean, I gave $20 to the Barack Obama Campaign and bought a bottle of water from those nuisance kids on the sidewalk. What more do you want from me?

Of course, I still believe in service to others. I am the youngest member of my local Meals on Wheels chapter, which I have been working with for 11 years. I love old people. I'll take them over some badass kids or trifling grown-ups any day. Seniors really need help, and anyone who truly needs help has my support.

I agree with Chris Rock: I don't defend the TTs for abandoning public service in our neediest neighborhoods, but I understand. Helping out should not be a battle. Life is too challenging already, and adding a frustrating, threatening, or fruitless volunteer experience is generally more than most Talented Tenthers can bear.

There you have it. Type 1 TTs could care less and are just trying to get theirs, and Type 2 TTs would love to volunteer and usually have volunteered in the past but feel the experience was too negative and not a good use of their valuable time. Either way, the Talented Tenthers of the 21st century have failed miserably in their mission to help the other 90 percent who are depending on us.

Is it that we're not interested? Is it some strange manifestation of self-hatred? Or have we become new-age Darwinists who simply believe in the survival of the fittest? Whatever the reason, our community loses out when the best and brightest turn their Armani-adorned backs on the less fortunate.

So what do we do now? The Talented Tenthers have lost interest, become disenchanted with public service. In some cases they just don't give a shit. What does this say for the future of the African American community? If we don't reach back to help one another, why should we expect others to help us? The nonprofit/service realm has long been dominated by white women, with no change in sight. I definitely know that I have to do more to give back, that Meals on Wheels just isn't enough.

We must elevate the notion of service in our communities and in our young people. We must require of ourselves and our neighbors a stronger commitment to volunteering and giving financially to those in need. We don't have to wait for a Hurricane Katrina in order to rally around those less fortunate. We can spend every day in search of opportunities to make the world a better place for those who come behind us.

I challenge us all to overcome our prejudices and reservations, lower our shoulders, and tackle the important needs of our communities. I know, I know, it ain't easy, but someone has to do it. We owe our ancestors that. Generations before fought and struggled and helped and gave for the betterment of the entire community so we could live the way we live now. This generation cannot break that chain. It would be a tragedy.

We must find services and causes that help those most in need but that don't drive us insane. Know who you are and what suits you best. If you're not a kid person, help old people. If you think old people smell funny, help kids or teach adults to read. If you hate everyone, work with animals. Find something you can enjoy doing and that makes you happy. But do SOMETHING. It will change you for the better. Everything isn't for everybody, and perhaps helping people beat the legal system just wasn't my thing. But there are plenty of other things I can do to fulfill my Talented Tenth obligations.

Most of us wouldn't be where we are today had someone not volunteered their time to help make our road through life a little smoother. We should return the favor for the next generation. Let's make our ancestors proud by reaching back to help those who need us most, even if it's not always easy.

Meanwhile, W. E. B. DuBois is probably turning over in his grave when he sees how his precious Talented Tenth turned out. He's checking us out, thinking what spoiled brats we are, what ungrateful SOBs we are. But on the other hand, you never know, he may be looking down and saying, "I don't blame them, I wouldn't put up with that bullshit either."

10

DOING THE BEST I CAN WITH WHAT I GOT

"When I discover who I am, I'll be free." —*Ralph Ellison*

No one is perfect or lives a perfect life, least of all me. Sometimes I ask myself, How can I run a site that tells people to do better and write a blog that reminds folks that *conversate* is not a word, when I have a past that would shock the conscience of most? Do I really have the right to tell anybody anything?

It is only by the grace of God that I have come this far. It is true that I have been in situations that could have easily derailed my life. It is true that I have been irresponsible, selfish, and reckless. Does that make me less able to challenge others to do better than I did? Is it wrong to ask my community to do better?

I don't know. I feel conflicted. I have made bad choices. At what point are you disqualified from challenging others to do better? Are you ever? I've learned from my mistakes. As a man once asked me, Is redemption possible? To that I would say yes. Throughout this journey, I have made it a point never to put myself on a pedestal, because, believe me, that's the last place I belong. I've never held myself up as a prototype or role model. I'm just a regular, fucked up, fatherless girl who happened to do OK for herself in this world. And I want us all to do OK for ourselves, and I want kids to have a world that encourages them to be their best, a world like the one I had.

I feel like I get it from both directions. People accuse me of being a privileged bourgeois Negro who looks down my nose at those less fortunate. Yet I've also been accused of being such a ne'er-do-well in my past that I don't have the right to tell others what to do. When either of these accusations arise I say this: my slogan is *we* got to do better. Not *y'all*. I am included in this. As incorrigible as I was at one time, the only thing that helped me through was the belief my parents instilled in me that I could be whatever I wanted to be, that I had limitless potential.

My household stressed education. And although some of the stuff I did after school could easily end up on hotghettomess.com, I never lost sight of my goals. There was a strange disconnect between my real life and my play life. As bad as I was, I was good when it counted. And that's only because of my upbringing. It's because my parents (who were not together but had a great friendship) did not accept Cs. Cs were average, and I wasn't average. And they told me that every day. My family and friends constantly challenged me to do better and held me up to high expectations. That's the sole reason I was able to survive and thrive.

And that's all I'm really saying here. There are some fundamental values that we can instill in the next generation that can carry them through the tumultuous times and the bad decisions they may make along their lives' journeys. We can't do that if we are too busy living for the moment. We can't do that if we're too busy trying to be rap stars. We can't do that if we're too busy keeping up with the Joneses (by the way, the Joneses are in foreclosure). We can't do that when our families are disintegrating. We can't do that if we're not stressing the importance of education. We can't do that if we don't show them loving relationships between partners. We can't do that when we have too many children with too many fathers and none of them are around. We can't do that when we continue to buy what we want and beg for what we need.

We must stop and recognize that many of our communities are headed in the wrong direction. Sure, it's hard to hear; sure, it's embarrassing and uncomfortable to confront this on the world's stage. But what is more important: avoiding embarrassment or attacking and solving our problems? Most people were upset at what Bill Cosby said not because it wasn't true but because he said it in public. As he would say, "Come on, people."

Perhaps my tactics could be refined. Perhaps I could be nicer and not use so many cuss words. I just practice tough love on my people. Consider me the mean parent of the community. Often you have one parent who is supportive and sweet, in whose eyes you can do no wrong. Then you have the other parent who makes you strip naked and then beats you in the street. I believe we need both. Can you imagine a child who is never told he or she is wrong? A child who is never told that he or she needs to get their act together? What would that child's future look like?

Sure, it's nice to hear what a rich history we have and how beautiful and capable and talented we are. Yes, it's wonderful to be told that we are the descendants of kings and queens. Yes, it's great to watch *Oprah* and read *Essence* and watch *Akeelah and the Bee* and revel in how fabulous we are. But eeeeeevery once in a while we also need a kick in the ass.

If we continue to believe that we are doing fine and any criticism of the community is racist drivel, then how do we progress? How do we improve? My friend the Wharton MBA business genius says his philosophy when talking about new ideas with someone is, "Don't tell me what's right about the idea, tell me what's wrong." Hearing what's wrong is often the way we learn. Often we are blinded by the love of ourselves and our communities. We are not all good, and we're not all bad. Sometimes there's a little of both. So why can't we talk about both?

Why can't we uplift the positive and denigrate the ignorant at the same time? It's like that old *In Living Color* sketch: "Y'all betta not say nuthin' bad about Ms. Jenkins." Except now it's "Y'all betta not say nuthin' bad about the black community." It's like everyone's ears immediately shut off at the merest hint that black people can do better than they are doing.

Please realize it is only out of concern and love that I challenge us to do better. I challenge myself to do better because I want to reach all of the potential my school teachers talked so much about on my report cards. I challenge my family and friends to do better because I know they can. I am contemptuous of apathy and mediocrity in all its forms, wherever it comes from. I really don't intend to be mean or nasty, but I get so frustrated and angry at missed opportunities. And I want everyone to get frustrated and angry because frustration and anger are often the inspiration for uprisings and social movements. Maybe it takes pissing everyone off to get people fired up.

But what about empathy and compassion? some ask. Where is my sensitivity?

Now I know if you've read this far, it could be easily construed that I have NO empathy in my heart, that my empathy well is bone-dry, as it were. Well, although that would make me a great Supreme Court Justice candidate, nothing could be further from the truth.

I am extremely empathetic. Hell, I'm a Pisces. We Pisces are famously empathetic and typically become absorbed in other people's issues to such an extreme that it's paralyzing. One day when you're looking for some light beach reading, check out Kurt Cobain's suicide letter. He was a Pisces too, and it's a perfect example of the crippling empathy those born under the sign of the fish are blessed with.

I'm no different. Beyond my rough and tumble exterior is a very warm and sensitive woman. I love old people and babies (except on airplanes and in restaurants) and animals. I cried when I saw *Ghost* just like everyone else. I want the best for everyone; I am compassionate and grateful. I strive for excellence and don't make excuses. I am very aware of my shortcomings and constantly try to improve.

I am all about empathy, but does empathy have a limit? Is there a point at which you can't empathize because you just don't get it? Do I really need to empathize with someone who acts like a victim even when he or she isn't? How do I empathize with someone who dismisses hard work in favor of a life of waiting on checks? How do I empathize with someone who doesn't take an active role in his or her children's education?

Believe me, I WANT to have empathy, but my visceral reaction is outrage when I'm confronted with a generation that is proving itself to be weak and expendable. We are descendants of the strongest of the strong. We have overcome all odds to get to where we are today. Our achievements in the 50 years since integration are extraordinary. So it pisses me off to no end when I look at opportunities squandered. Dreams voluntarily deferred. It's like fumbling the ball on first and goal.

So it's not that I am incapable of empathy and sensitivity. I just feel that empathy has a limit. I feel like I'm on that show *Intervention* and the black community is the meth-head son—I don't want to kick him out because I'm afraid he'll be killed, so I allow him to stay with me because at least I'll know where he is even if it means a life of him cussing me out, beating up my other kids, and stealing my shit. There is a fine line between empathy and enabling. I know. I've had my toe on that line.

I do believe we all could benefit from a greater spirit of empathy. However, empathy and a sincere concern for others shouldn't ever be manipulated to advance anyone's agenda. I think everyone would agree with that. So why does it make me some sort of cold-hearted monster to say it out loud? It doesn't.

The world has become hard and cold and selfish and people have generally followed suit, which is a bad thing. To combat this lack of warmth in the world, I'm torn between being warmer and being colder.

I just yearn so badly for the day when our communities can be self-sufficient. When you can do for yourself, you can approach the world on your terms. You can use the world to enhance your life as opposed to depending on it for your survival. That's what I want for the black community and for all Americans. Let's fight for the big things. Let's not get bogged down in begging for scraps when most of us are perfectly capable of making it on our own. Let's fight racism, sexism, substandard education, discrimination, and harmful public policies. Those are the fights that collectively advance us.

The rest we can handle. We should get a firm grip on all those aspects of our lives that we *can* control and use the dogged determination that got us this far to keep pressing forward. We must fight for our families and morality and standards and decency and integrity. No election will deliver us that. We must set our sights on excellence as a common goal and hold each other accountable. We must do the best we can with what we have.

I don't want the empathy well to run dry. Too many deserving people need a helping hand. But we jeopardize those folks who really need help when we become the group that cried wolf. We make such a big fuss about bullshit most of the time that the world begins to tune us out. We'll come to be seen as whiners. So when there is a fight that's really worth taking on, no one will pay us any mind.

Competence and excellence are the solutions to racism, not more programs. More money into people's hands isn't necessarily the answer, either—look at all the idiots who win the lottery and end up flat broke in two years. The desire to be captains of our own destinies will promote change. Having vision and goals and a thirst for excellence will place us and our needs on the world's radar.

We must begin by looking at ourselves in the mirror. And not the Mary J. Blige, walking-past-the-mirror look, but the sit-in-the-mirror-and-examine-ourselves-closely look. Like when you were a teenager and you were scouring your reflection for the first signs of a zit. We must all take a second, look at the world, and then look at ourselves. Where do we fit in?

Steven Friedman wrote the book *The World Is Flat*. In it, he talks about a new world in which globalization and technology have leveled the playing field. So where do we see ourselves in this new flat world?

It is incumbent on us all to take advantage of the opportunities available to make our lives better. We must ensure a new generation of young people will have minds and visions as expansive as their tennis shoe collections and tattoos. The limits to our existence often exist only in our minds. We place our energy into all the wrong things. The things we can do, we must do.

For example, many of us feel that travel is something we see only in flashy music videos. Too many of us will spend hundreds renting out a local banquet hall for a party or a cabaret but have never left the city, or worse, the south side of town. We should use that much energy gathering ourselves and our children up and driving a few hours in any direction. Spend the weekend in a place you've never been. Sometimes you have to remind yourself how large the world is. We get so caught up in our little bubbles that we forget how expansive our lives can be. Show yourself and your children the sunrise from a mountain, or an ancient American Indian burial ground, or a green pasture every now and then.

Traveling beyond your block and your comfort zone leads to a broader worldview. It reminds you that there is so much more out there besides the banal problems of urban living. It shows your children that the world is a big place, that they are not tethered to their hood and its limitations. Show them kids who speak different languages, play different games, and listen to different music. City kids, country kids. Kids who have never heard gunshots at night. Kids who play the piano and act in plays. Kids whose lives are far more difficult than theirs. Challenge the myopic view many of our children have of their lives, their potential, and their place in the world. Take a break and get away from the routines of your life for a day or two. When you are sitting around a campfire with your children, noisy neighbors, a pain-in-the-ass boss, love handles, and your cell phone bill just don't seem that important.

And even if a campfire or road trip is beyond your reach, there is always the other side of town. There are always the museum programs and library readings and cultural festivals that give you a brief escape from your reality. You are reminded of how dynamic the world is if you just take the time to explore it.

A broad worldview is so important, especially for children. I have good friends who participated in a busing program in the '80s. They tell me that being exposed to a better school wasn't necessarily beneficial to them, but being exposed to a different life, different people, and different possibilities was. It wasn't the algebra classes but the life lessons they learned that were invaluable.

And this type of exposure is within everyone's reach. It just takes thought, sacrifice, and a reexamination of our priorities.

We have to begin to think of ourselves as integral parts of this new global society. For so long we have sat on the sidelines and watched the action, believing that real involvement and influence were just beyond our reach. In the age of Obama and media convergence and hedge funds, we must start acting like the extraordinary community we are and take our place among the guiders of this new millennium.

As I said earlier, language will play an integral role in shaping our world over the next century. And I don't mean splitting verbs, right place–right time language. I mean learning another language.

Now I know that, as Americans, we are predisposed to ethnocentricity and believe that everyone should just speak English, but we have to stop fooling ourselves. Not only will a second language be a practical necessity soon, but it is also a valuable asset in the job market. The demographics of the country are rapidly changing, and the lack of importance many urban communities place on learning a second language is extraordinary.

I remember when I worked as a server in a downtown restaurant. Most of the servers and management staff were African American, and most of the support staff (i.e., busboys, dishwashers, and food runners) were Latino. We all used to giggle at their broken English and get super frustrated when they didn't understand. We used to say sexually suggestive things to them, thinking they wouldn't catch on. In other words, we were just some dumb-ass kids. But I'll never forget my manager saying to us as he heard us giggling, "They can understand you, but you can't understand them." Here we were, a bunch of silly, misguided young adults who spent all our tip money on drinking and partying, laughing at a staff of Latino men who all worked two jobs and had a better work ethic than all of us put together. And maybe their English wasn't great, but it was definitely better than our Spanish.

It's funny, I see some of those guys today, years later, and we always laugh about the good old days at the restaurant. And trust me when I tell you that their English now is better than some of my college students'. And I still don't know Spanish. But at least I'm trying to learn.

It always grates my nerves when I see young people making fun of the Korean manicurist or the Indian convenience store owner or the Chinese carry-out owner. I always want to say, "These people have come from other countries and have managed to start businesses and get educations often without even having a grasp of the English language. What have *you* done, young brother? How is your Korean?"

My point, and I do have one, is that focusing on language skills doesn't take money. Foreign languages *are* taught in public schools. But you must stress the importance of that education to your children. Work on it with them. There are inexpensive computer programs that the whole family can use. There are even free podcasts with Spanish lessons. Instead of watching *For the Love of Ray J* one night, do a Spanish tutorial with your children. You and your kids will both be better for it. We have the resources, and we must make it a priority. Pronto.

And yes, I mentioned a computer at home. Now I know everyone doesn't have a home computer, but I would argue that for many, it's once again about priorities. How do you have a DVD player and TVs in all your car headrests and no computer in your home? How do you have

$3,000 rims and no e-mail address? Why would you spend $800 on a weave when, for the same amount, you can get a PC?

The Digital Divide is a term used to describe the lack of techno-logical access among the poor, minority populations, and those in rural areas. The Digital Divide theory posits that as the Internet becomes increasingly integral to America's cultural, social, and economic way of life, those on the wrong side of the divide, also known as the other side of the tracks, will be further disenfranchised. We must understand this and work to use available resources to bridge that gap.

As a people, we've always been ingenious. A culture that can make classic dishes out of discarded scraps of food and music from two turn-tables and a microphone surely can figure out how to get online and stay there. We must bring our innovative spirit to the cyberworld. And I don't just mean celebrity gossip or the booty pics on Black Planet. Expanding our worldview must also include the acceptance of computer and media literacy as a vital part of our growth as a culture. If you can figure out how to work that two-pound remote that combines your sur-round sound, satellite, X-Box, iPod, and Blu-Ray player, you can get your ass online.

When I say we must do the best we can with what we have, it means that excellence isn't about money. It's about embracing life and striving for achievement and competence. In this day and age, competence is invaluable. I know that sounds very Booker T. Washington-esque, but without hard work and competence, we can't compete for a piece of the pie. Even if the playing field isn't always level, we certainly can't stake a claim to the American dream while sitting on our asses. The same goes for people of every race and class. Once you assume the victim role, the helpless citizen, the lost child of history, you are dooming yourself to irrelevance.

We have all the tools to excel, to create healthy families, and to foster thriving communities. Admittedly, some are born with the deck stacked against them and some simply make mistakes along the way. Those are the brothers and sisters who deserve our empathy, our compassion, our help. But it's getting harder to distinguish between those who really need help and those who really need an ass kicking.

The tools for success are within our reach. The keys to the kingdom are right before our eyes if we would just open them behind our Dolce & Gabbana shades. Seeing lost opportunities and squandered potential is frustrating, and at times I do get angry and exasperated.

I feel like I've been burned once. I went into the community and tried to help my ass off, but I just got, as my mother would say, "Screwed without a kiss." (I come from a very liberal family.) And that wasn't some isolated incident. My coworkers felt the same way, my colleagues at similar programs felt the same way, and the people who e-mail me every day feel the same way. We all want to help. But it's hard to stay motivated when 80 percent of your caseload is scam artists who are perfectly content sucking at the government's tit until they can't suck anymore.

In the end, I'm conflicted and discontented. I only want the best for my community. I love my people, but they drive me absolutely ape-shit sometimes. I know my tactics are controversial and my methodology is harsh. Well, it may be harsh, but it is mine. My goal is to start a movement where communities become the driving force for promoting accountability, responsibility, and higher standards. No government program can give you the desire to improve your life. No social worker can tell you how to dream big and have a vision beyond your current reality. It is up to us to grab all the opportunities and all the knowledge we can so we can thrive. As a result, the community as a whole will thrive. But progress requires (1) recognizing the problem, and (2) ACTION.

We all have a role to play in being the best citizens we can. We need to make better decisions with regard to parenthood and relationships and finances and work and education and sexuality. Period. It doesn't matter how much money a government program spends on you if you continue to make decisions that hold you back. So what if the federal government makes college more affordable if you drop out of high school? We can't continue to run away from the profound consequences our bad choices have had on our communities and our children by blaming everyone else.

The government can't legislate pride in ourselves. We can't picket for appropriate standards of behavior in our communities. Boycotts and letter-writing campaigns will not stop our young men and women from going to proms dressed like pimps and prostitutes. A congressional hearing won't make men be fathers and won't make women more responsible when they're deciding whom to have children with. The reactionary, hysterical, white-people-save-us-from-ourselves/blame-game mode of social change is so tired.

If we don't stand up and say that certain destructive behaviors are unacceptable—spending more money on clothes and cars than a home is unacceptable, having two or three kids with two or three people is unacceptable, not stressing education in your home is unacceptable, listening to certain songs on the radio is unacceptable, neglecting your kids is unacceptable, stepping over the trash in front of your door instead of picking that shit up is unacceptable, not being able to say a sentence without splitting a verb is unacceptable—then who will?

You gotta call a spade a spade, and sometimes you gotta call a hot ghetto mess a hot ghetto mess. And until we get it together, I will keep calling us out when we don't represent our communities well. I'll leave the positivity and sunshine and light to *Essence* and Oprah and *Black Enterprise*.

Mine is but one voice in the pantheon of approaches to social change. It's not THE solution, but it's part of it. It's time for us to be honest with ourselves. It doesn't matter what you think about me as long as when you put this book down, you think about how you can do better in your life, in your community, and in the lives of our children. If that happens, then my efforts will not have been in vain. Look, all we got is us, and if we don't love each other enough to give tough love, to call each other out, and to challenge ourselves to do better, then who will?

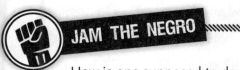

JAM THE NEGRO

How is one supposed to do the best they can with what they got when they don't have anything?!? You talk all this big talk but never stop to consider that families who are barely getting by don't have time to ponder a broad worldview or Booker T. Washington or anything else. When you spend every moment scratching and scraping, it's hard to see much further than your circumstance. All your talk sounds real purty and Oprah-like, but when are you going to join the rest of your community in the real world? Take a drive to a meadow? You must be out your damn head. You think I want to drive to some scenic location so I can hear my kids complain about how there's no TV and no video games and nothing to do? I work too hard to set myself up for that shit. I'd much rather go to a cabaret down at the reception hall than drag my badass kids anywhere. I know that sounds mean, but my whole life is about them. What about me? And, whether you want to believe it or not, a lot of people ARE about excellence. I get my hair and nails done every two weeks; I wear nice clothes; and my children have all the newest designers and games. I believe in being first class at all times. My kids aren't failing any classes in school, and they all are going to graduate from high school, so you can take your preaching to someone who cares, Miss Thang. I don't care if you have empathy for me or not. Just like I won't have empathy when you lose everything in your 401(k) when the economy goes down the crapper again. You kill me with all your reaching-for-the-stars bullshit. When I get home from busting my ass for 13 hours, the only thing I want to reach for is a beer. I'm tired of you blaming me, because

I'm the one who is oppressed. I'm the one who has terrible schools in my neighborhood, no job opportunities, and no adequate housing or government services. Why don't you demand excellence of them? Why don't you demand that the government give ME some excellence for a damn change? You're always looking in the wrong direction, at people who are willing to speak out. Like me.

JAM THE AMERICAN

(SIGH)
Peace, people.

EPILOGUE

JAM THE NEGRO

Well, that was just about the worst piece of anti-black crap I have ever read. You can pretend that all your abuse and tough, anti-black talk comes from love, but I know better. You are just an elitist, privileged asshole who probably gets great joy at making fun of people and chastising your own community like they're children. Well, we're not children, and we don't need a lecture from the likes of you. People get a little education and suddenly they think they have all the answers and want to dictate how everyone else should live their lives. I refuse to be lectured. Maybe once you stand up for something real—protest something or march for something— maybe then you'll have some credibility. You probably weren't even at the Jena Six rally. You're just a bunch of hot air. You and your kind.

You think you're actually helping? By giving racists ammunition and confirming their worst fears about us? You really think that's helpful? Perpetuating stereotypes? You are so misguided. Why don't you highlight what's good in our communities instead of focusing on what's bad and painting an unbalanced picture of how we live? We are bombarded by negative images from the mainstream media all day, every day, and now you come along and pile on. What's shocking is that you think you are providing some sort of service. That you believe this sort of talk and these types of images are promoting some sort of social change is a true indication that you are certifiably nuts. I just hope that one day you open your eyes.

People need to be uplifted, not put down. People are doing bad, not because they don't want to succeed, but because they just don't have the opportunities that others have. It's not their fault. This country makes it hard for poor people and people of color to get ahead. Racism is a part of so many institutions in this country. Maybe if you open your eyes you would see that. You're so busy blaming black people for their own problems that you don't see the big picture. Look at the criminal justice system. You think it's an accident that so many black men are in jail? Just look at those racist crack laws.

This country will never allow people of color to get ahead. Sure, some progress has been made, but it's because we had the courage to fight for what the country owed us for 400 years of free labor. We must continue to fight for our piece of the pie. Unfortunately, people like you want us to sit back and buy this color-blind, human race bullshit. You want us to forget about our history and be good little Americans and not rock the boat. Well, fat chance. While you're so busy worrying about what's going on in our communities, you need to be worried about what this country is systematically doing to people of color every day. Can you say Rodney King or Henry Louis Gates? I guess them getting beat down and arrested and treated as second-class citizens was their fault too? Look lady, have you ever heard of loyalty? We have to stick together, and we can't do that when people like you are undermining the community. So you can take your sucky little book, your cuss words, your fake concern, and your race-hating vitriol and stick it where the sun don't shine. With friends like you, who needs enemies? Peace, my ass.

JAM THE AMERICAN

It's unfortunate that we would rather save face than save lives. You can talk about me all you want, and you can call me every name in the book. I really don't care. I just say what most people are thinking. And until we have the balls to get together and have a real, honest, and uncomfortable conversation about our communities and what's going on in them, we will never solve the problems. But I guess to some people it doesn't matter. As long as we have the government, the CIA, hip-hop, and BET to blame all of our problems on, everything will be fine. Because it's easy to picket BET and Don Imus and Ludacris. What's hard is looking each other in the eye and asking, What role do we play in this? It's easy to call me an Uncle Tom for posting pictures of girls dressing like whores at their proms. It's harder to confront parents and chaperones and principals and ask them why they allowed it to happen in their homes and schools.

We have to bypass the low-hanging fruit and feigned outrage and get to the crux of the issues. Is there racism in the criminal justice system and education and financial institutions and the media? Of course. But knowing that the deck is stacked against you makes it imperative that you navigate the system with that in mind. Play the system. You can't let it play you. While we protest racist crack laws, let's tell our young people not to sell it. If you know economic opportunities are scarce in the inner city, why make it more difficult by dropping out of school? We cannot profess to know the system and its faults so well yet keep allowing it to play us. We dress like pimps and hos and then complain that we are stereotyped as pimps and hos. We claim to know all the tricks, yet instead of avoiding them, we continue to fall right into them and then complain they were there. It's time to advance to the next level: a state of self-sufficiency, empowerment, and true community. And like any other issue, the first step in solving the problem is recognizing you have one. We all know we have massive problems that only we can solve, and pretending that it's not true will not make them go away.

So you can be mad at me all you want. You and all the rest of the outrage addicts, poverty pimps, and victim valiants can go on about Mumia and reparations and Tupac, acting like helpless victims whose progress in life is determined solely by the whims of the white man. Meanwhile, the rest of us will reach for our dreams knowing that the only thing holding us back is ourselves. I know for a fact that we all are capable of success beyond our wildest expectations, and no one is capable of dashing your dreams except you. I will always hold myself and everyone else to high expectations and high standards, and I will continue to hold my brothers and sisters accountable for any behavior they may engage in that is detrimental to us as a community. I refuse to back down. So for the black thought Nazis whose thinking has not progressed in the last 30 years: Negroes, please.

INDEX

ABOUT THE AUTHOR

JAM DONALDSON is the managing editor of the online news-magazine Blackpower.com, the creator of the popular Web site hotghettomess.com, and the writer and producer of the BET series *We Got to Do Better*. As an attorney, Donaldson has received the Frederick Abramson Award for Public Service. A visiting professor at Morgan State University in Baltimore, she lives in Washington, D.C.

I Didn't Work This Hard Just to Get Married

Successful Single Black Women Speak Out

by Nika C. Beamon

978-1-55652-819-4
$14.95 (CAN $16.95)

"Presents interviews with 21 successful black women fully enjoying single-hood with a range of opinions on their marriage prospects. . . . The women applaud the television shows *Living Single* and *Girlfriends* for depictions of beautiful and successful single black women, and discuss the sometimes negative images of black women and the impact of the high unemployment and incarceration rates of black men on marriage prospects. Mostly, they recount their own personal journeys to accepting, enjoying, and capitalizing on their times as single women." —*Booklist*

Women once saw living single as a transitional period—singles marked time till they found "the one." But now marriage is the transitional stage, connecting one unmarried period of life to another. In *I Didn't Work This Hard Just to Get Married*, through lively and revealing interviews with women from various walks of life, Nika C. Beamon explores the challenges facing single black women who defy expectations. They candidly discuss aging without a man and reevaluate dating, single homeownership, careers, children, and caring for aged parents. Written in the best tradition of women talking to women, and girlfriend to girlfriend, the book delivers tales of lessons learned, hard times and good times, told by women who found ways to achieve their dreams by defying convention.

Not All Black Girls Know How to Eat

A Story of Bulimia

Not All Black Girls Know How to Eat
A Story of Bulimia

by Stephanie Covington Armstrong

978-1-55652-786-9
$16.95 (CAN $18.95)

"Enriches the genre of eating disorder narratives by diversifying the chorus of voices. Covington Armstrong's story emboldens women of all colors who might otherwise have remained quiet to voice their lived experiences with food." —*Ms.*

With a childhood defined by poverty, hunger, foster care, and sexual abuse, Stephanie Covington Armstrong does not fit the stereotype of a woman with an eating disorder. In this insightful and moving first-person narrative, Armstrong describes her struggle as a black woman with a disorder that is consistently portrayed as a white woman's problem. Stephanie tries to escape her self-hatred and her food obsession by never slowing down, unaware that she is caught in a downward spiral emotionally, spiritually, and physically. Finally, she can no longer deny that she will die if she doesn't get help, overcome her shame, and conquer her addiction to using food as a weapon against herself.

Lawrence Hill Books

Available at your favorite bookstore or at
www.lawrencehillbooks.com